SCHOLASTIC

GRADES 3–5

READ-ALOUDS WITH HEART

Literacy Lessons That Build Community, Comprehension, and Cultural Competency

DANA CLARK, KEISHA SMITH-CARRINGTON, AND JIGISHA VYAS

Scholastic Inc. grants teachers permission to print and photocopy the reproducible pages from this book for classroom use. Purchase of this book entitles use of reproducibles by one teacher for one classroom only. No other part of this publication may be reproduced in whole or in part, or stored in a retrieval system, or transmitted in any form or by any means, electronic, mechanical, photocopying, recording, or otherwise, without written permission of the publisher. For information regarding permission, write to Scholastic Inc., 557 Broadway, New York, NY 10012.

SVP and Publisher: Tara Welty
Editor: Maria L. Chang
Cover design: Cynthia Ng
Interior design: Michelle H. Kim
Cover illustration: Shutterstock Inc.
Photos: Courtesy of the authors
Icons: Noun Project

ISBN: 978-1-338-86191-4
Scholastic Inc., 557 Broadway, New York, NY 10012
Copyright © 2023 by Dana Clark, Keisha Smith-Carrington, and Jigisha Vyas
Published by Scholastic Inc. All rights reserved.
Printed in the U.S.A.
First printing, March 2023.
1 2 3 4 5 6 7 8 9 10   40   30 29 28 27 26 25 24 23

TABLE OF CONTENTS

Letter From the Authors..5

The Learning Part..7
    Learning About Ourselves...15
    Learning About Our Practices..33

The Lessons Part...59
    All the Way to the Top...64
    Birdsong..68
    Digging for Words..72
    Dreamers..76
    Fauja Singh Keeps Going...80
    The Fearless Flights of Hazel Ying Lee......................................84
    In Our Mothers' House..88
    The Journey..93
    Mango Moon...97
    Pride..102
    The Proudest Blue..106
    Separate Is Never Equal...111
    The Case for Loving..115
    Watercress..119
    We Are Water Protectors...124
    Your Name Is a Song...128

The Final Part...132
    Notes From the Authors..135
    Acknowledgments..138
    Resources...141

Dear Reader,

The book you now hold in your hands started as a seed of hope and a conversation between Dana (a White, cisgender woman), Jigisha (a Southeast Indian, cisgender woman), and Keisha (a Black, cisgender woman). Little by little, that seed was nurtured as the three of us brought together our dream of classrooms in which every student feels seen, valued, and loved. Together, we imagined spaces where learning centers multiple perspectives and celebrates collective knowledge, rather than competition. We imagined a space that would allow students to succeed as learners because their emotional needs were met first. We imagined interdependent communities working to ensure the holistic success of each member so the whole could thrive. We hoped, we came together, we envisioned, we imagined . . . and we studied. Our seed of hope grew as we began to formulate ways to co-create environments and learn with students in a classroom, resources to use, and lessons to teach. That became this book, which lays out our pathway to the classrooms we've been dreaming of.

On the surface, it may seem like this book is about mentor texts, but the reality is that it is way more than that. It is about creating a classroom community that centers students: honoring the identities of everyone in the room, undertaking thoughtful and empathetic reading, and engaging in action that strengthens the humanity of each member. We understand that you may be tempted to jump straight to the mentor texts and lessons. But in order to prepare to bring the beautiful books and lessons we describe into your work with students, you must first do work with yourself. We have learned that conversations around identity require that we study not only learning structures that will support students' social and emotional learning but also how our identities impact our ways of being with students.

It is our intention that the first part of this book act as both a guide and a journal so that you can dream up your own vision of the classroom you hope to create and get clarity on where your own identity journey begins. To that end, this foundational part has two distinct purposes. The Learning About Ourselves section is designed to act as a mirror—opening the door to reflective activities that invite you to analyze the ways you look at and respond to yourself and others who are and are not like you. In subsequent sections, activities and topics designed to help you bring a reflective stance to that reading are tagged with a little journal icon. The Learning About Our Practices section offers windows into possible practices that support community and literacy learning. This includes reading lenses and ideas on strategy instruction, tips on using circle practices to support learning, and ways to coach your readers as they transfer their learning into their own choice reading.

The Lessons Part of this book is designed as a menu. Choose a book. Choose a strategy. Choose a standard. Create your own adventure. While we do offer some possibilities on how to make these choices, there isn't a right or wrong way to bring the stories and lesson work into your classroom community. Our hope is that you can find the learning, books, and conversations that speak to you and help guide the next steps you take with your learners.

The Final Part speaks to ways you can move beyond our book recommendations to transfer our lenses and ideas to self-selected titles. Here, you will also find a personalized note from each of us.

Oh, and one last thing before you really dig in. One main tenet of this work is our belief in community. That belief extends beyond our classrooms. We believe that teaching and professional learning is also best done in community. While the beginning sections include reflection pages that will allow you to sit with yourself to reflect and imagine, we hope that you won't have to do this alone. We suggest you find a thinking partner who can support you through this first section. However, if you are on your own, please be sure to lean into some of the accompanying resources—and know that we are here with you, too.

Yours in learning and community,
Dana, Keisha, and Jigisha

Bonus online materials: To access additional mini-lessons and other resources, go to www.scholastic.com/readaloudswithheart and enter this password: **SC747201**.

THE LEARNING PART

Decades ago, in her powerful essay "Mirrors, Windows, and Sliding Glass Doors," Rudine Sims Bishop shared the importance of building classroom libraries in which all students can see themselves and their families in the pages of a book. She wrote: "When children cannot find themselves reflected in the books they read, or the images they see are distorted, negative, or laughable, they learn a powerful lesson on how they are devalued in the society of which they are a part" (1990). Every student deserves to feel acknowledged and valued in our classrooms. And yet more than 30 years after Bishop wrote those words, the representation of all children in our libraries and mentor texts is still lacking.

Since 1985, the Cooperative Children's Book Center (CCBC) has documented the number of books by and about Black people. In 1994, they added books by and about Indigenous and other People of Color to their statistics. In 2018, the CCBC also began collecting statistics for additional identities, such as LGBT+, disability, and religion. As the Diversity in Children's Books 2018 graphic below shows, we cannot depend upon the publishing industry to ensure that the faces our students see as they turn the pages of a book will match their own faces or those of the children sitting around them.

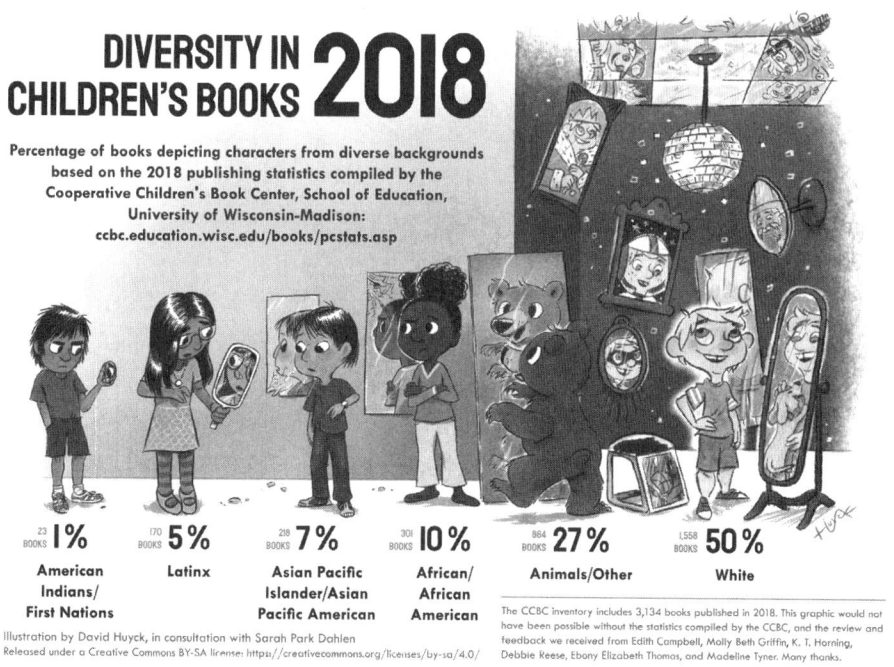

While efforts over the past few years have increased representation across Black, Indigenous, and other People of Color (BIPOC), these groups are still woefully underrepresented in children's books. The responsibility to make sure that our classroom libraries and mentor texts provide students with window, mirror, and sliding glass door experiences falls on us as educators. Truly, there is no reason for our school libraries or classroom libraries to look like the image above. For this reason, Keisha works tirelessly with teachers, school librarians, and achievement coaches to create diverse collections in all the elementary and middle school spaces in her district. She also helps educators develop and strengthen the skills, knowledge, and dispositions they need to facilitate their and their students' cultural competence through literacy, inclusive not only of the strands of reading, writing, speaking, listening, and language, but also of critical literacy, gender literacy, and racial literacy.

We cannot stop at simply putting "diverse books" on our library shelves. First, as Chad Everett, chief instructional officer at Imaginelit.com, clearly explained in a blog post, "There is no diverse book" (2017). Using "[the] word *diverse* as it is currently used centers heteronormative whiteness as the default . . . labeling any single text as diverse stands in direct contradiction to the intended purpose of the call for diverse texts. A binary lens of diversity only further *others* the narratives of individuals from minoritized groups." This argument can be used to support the years of research by the CCBC, which has included and expanded the number of backgrounds, both minoritized and normalized, in its quantifications of diversity in publishing.

Second, it is not sufficient for the books to simply occupy space in rooms with children who may neither select nor have the capacity to fully comprehend stories that provide windows and sliding glass doors (Bishop, 1990). Children deserve expansive conversations about how identities shape the ways we read books and see the world. We who teach reading are familiar with the work of Louise Rosenblatt, whose transactional theory details the way a reader's identity shapes comprehension of a text (1986). This transaction, in which the reader brings the self while examining a text, is the point at which the text may be labeled as diverse for that individual reader (Rosenblatt, 2017).

Through deep and purposeful experiences with texts, students can learn and practice ways to explore their identity and build empathy for people with different identities. By intentionally curating collections that represent many group identities for both mini-lessons and choice reading, teachers provide students with opportunities to strengthen self- and social awareness and to engage in deep thinking and discourse that can increase competency in self-management, relationship skills, and responsible decision-making. These five competencies of social-emotional learning (SEL) "enhance" English language arts/literacy curricula (CASEL, 2017a). They also dovetail with the social justice standards (see page 18).

Anchoring Our Practice: Books Are the Key

In The Lessons Part of this book (starting on page 59), you will find thoughtfully chosen mentor texts that bring young readers stories of celebration, hardship, love, and loss. We have chosen to center a few of our favorite texts within this resource because we know that books can spark conversations that need to be had in our classrooms—conversations that may be uncomfortable or that we've been afraid to have because we aren't sure how to start them. Books allow us to lean on the words and pictures of authors and illustrators and invite students into thinking together.

Books are key to this work. We also know that as wonderful as interactive read-alouds can be, books alone are not the answer. We have found that teachers sometimes neglect the follow-up small-peer group work and individual work with texts that truly cement learning. So, along with the mentor text suggestions and information about the books themselves, we provide mini-lessons that offer a choice of strategies, circle questions, and carryover coaching prompts for independence that will bring important conversations to life in the classroom.

The strategies and prompts laid out in the book use three "reading lenses" to deepen students' understanding of texts and people: Identity, Harm and Healing, and Heartwork. Through these lenses, students sharpen reading comprehension skills, such as analyzing character, determining themes, and exploring perspectives. They also find their way to apply new understandings to their everyday interactions with one another.

Table 1: Reading Lenses

Identity	Harm & Healing	Heartwork
The Identity work invites students to see characters as complex people who have layers—some chosen and some they were born with. These layers of identity blend together in each person to create a uniqueness of humanity.	Inspired by restorative practices, the work of this lens focuses on studying problems, resolutions, and themes. Stories, both real and imagined, often center people's struggles and the pathways they find to healing—pathways that can teach us all a lot about life.	The lens of Heartwork explores how readers can connect to the emotions of the characters and allow the stories to touch their hearts by noticing details and sharing perspectives.
We study: • how the identities of characters are revealed. • how identity connects to motivation, needs, desires, and actions. • how reading through our own identities and experiences influences our thinking and connections to characters.	**We study:** • how to identify internal and external struggles. • how to bring different perspectives to the problems in the text. • how struggles impact and motivate characters. • how to extract life lessons through the characters' responses to challenges.	**We study:** • how to take on the perspective of the characters. • how exploring different perspectives helps us gather more complex understandings of characters. • how word choice and images help readers identify mood and tone. • how empathy can help us live differently.

Why Identity?

Before answering "why identity?", let's first explore this question: What is identity? Author and literacy leader Gholdy Muhammad defines identify as: "notions of who we are, who others say we are (in both positive and negative ways), and whom we desire to be" (Muhammad, 2020). Author and professor Janet Sauer shares that identity is shaped as "a person identifies with a set of characteristics and holds beliefs about his or her related performances" (Sauer, 2014). Scholar and feminist writer Sara Ahmed describes our identities as "the many factors that shape who we are" (Ahmed, 2018).

Our hearts call out a big YES to each definition. We view identities as the collection of characteristics, beliefs, circumstances, and personal truths that make up each one of us. Our identities are constructed from the ways others see us and the ways we see ourselves.

Some aspects of our identity are predetermined: the parts of ourselves we are born with—brown skin, green eyes, curly hair. Other layers of identity build up and change as we live our lives. They may be influenced by our families, friends, neighborhoods, and experiences. These layers of our identities can be made up of things such as interests, objects and places that bring us joy, family traditions, and spiritual beliefs and practices.

Why should we bring identity study into reading? When we don't think

Readers bring their own identities into their reading—their identities affect how they think about a story and what they learn from it.

about our own identities and study the identities of the characters, we lose the opportunity to create meaning and truly understand the characters in our books. This leads us back to Louise Rosenblatt's transactional reader-response theory, which teaches that there is never a singular meaning of a text. When the words on the page and our lives come together, we construct meaning. Simply said, who we are impacts how we see the characters in our books, what we think about them and their choices, and what lessons we pull from the pages. That meaning can even change over time because our identities are not static. This is often the reason why when we reread a book that has sat on a bookshelf for years, it touches us differently. We may connect with a different character or see motivation with new eyes—maybe because we now look through the eyes of a caregiver or of someone who has experienced deep and devastating loss.

Dana remembers experiencing this with Shel Silverstein's *The Giving Tree*. Her view of the character of the tree changed with life and her shifting identities. In her youth, Dana saw the tree as simple and weak. Then, through the eyes of a new mother, she understood the tree's desire to give the boy the world, even if it meant sacrificing everything. Now, as the mom of two middle schoolers, she has the urge to call out to the tree and will her the strength to say no. Nothing in this book has changed. But life has shifted Dana's view and, in turn, the meaning that she takes from its pages.

We also believe that centering our students' identities in our classrooms and our libraries will connect them to books and one another. During a visit with a fifth-grade class, Dana saw students "tasting" some picture books that they might read during their upcoming unit. When one little girl saw the beautiful book *The Proudest Blue* by Ibtihaj Muhammad and S. K. Ali, she yelled out, "I want this one. She looks just like me." Dana recalls the joy that radiated from this student's face as she saw someone on the book's cover who looked like her and her family. You may have a similar story of students who were drawn to books that offered them a mirror. Our book collections must capture the identities of our students and offer books with characters who have very different identities as well.

Throughout her childhood, Jigisha recalls scanning the library shelves in search of a story that would spark her interest and inspire a joy of reading. She saw other children open pages of a book and immediately immerse themselves in the story. Jigisha, however, never found stories that she could see herself in or feel a sense of belonging to, or books that had characters who even looked like her. Then, in Jigisha's fourth year of teaching, her school welcomed author Sarah Weeks, who had come to share her book *Save Me a Seat*, which she wrote with Gita Varadarajan. Weeks spoke about how her coauthor's own experiences inspired the experiences of the main character. People regularly mispronounced Varadarajan's name, and the author often felt pressure to fit into a culture and experience that was different from her own.

Jigisha realized that in her entire life she had never experienced a deep connection with a story, a character, and an author until then—when she was already in her 20s. She had finally found a book that not only reflected her own upbringing but also connected to her role as an educator. She had missed this type of immersive experience throughout her childhood. Moments such as these underscore the powerful impact such an experience can have for many children. A book brings shared experiences to life, and educators can spark that joy for many.

Reading through the lens of Identity will help readers see how their perspectives and selves impact the story they experience. And beyond that, as they consider the identities that the characters carry into their thinking, readers will push themselves to see the complexities of the people in their books. These complexities can help them make sense of someone's circumstance, desire, or decision.

Why Harm and Healing?
As we scan the books on our shelves, we'd be hard-pressed to find one that doesn't present a problem. Maybe it's because without challenge, there is no story. Maybe it's because our greatest successes often result from overcoming struggles. Maybe it's because harm and healing can set in motion the cycle of learning to be better.

The name of this section, specifically the word *harm*, may seem harsh. After all, the word itself means "physical or emotional injury." We spent quite a bit of time considering whether to revise the name of this lens. We revisited the language time and time again, asking ourselves if it was right for an elementary-focused book. We thought about other words, such as *hurt* or *problem*. Yet in the end, none of those words really captured the heart of this work. *Harm* is a harsh word, but it is also something that happens to all of us.

Being human means that we will experience harm. Sometimes a person may do us harm. At best, it is someone we don't know well. At worst, it is someone whom we love. There are even times when we harm ourselves. Other times, the norms and systems of our society or the realities of our circumstances cause us pain. In the end, we chose *harm* because there is a responsibility tied to that word that doesn't exist in words like *problem* or *hurt*. During our lives, we will all be harmed, and we will all carry the burden of being responsible for harming someone else. *Harm* is the right word, but in our title it doesn't stand alone. Right next to it is the word *healing*. This lens sets out to help students identify when harm happens and then study how people move forward to heal.

Raising a generation of people who will preserve our planet, respect one another, and create a better world requires that we teach our students to look for the causes of conflict, the repercussions of harmful choices, AND the ways we might heal the hurt we have caused. If we focus on the challenges characters experience and the ways they find a way forward to heal, we can help our readers deepen their understanding of the story and be moved to make different choices themselves.

Why Heartwork?
We exist in a world divided. Lines drawn come in many shapes and colors—based on politics, beliefs, and desires. It is easy to focus on our differences and to allow ourselves to "other" people around us. But we don't have to do that. In practicing perspective sharing and opening ourselves up to someone else's truth, we can begin to erase the lines that divide us and teach our students to do the same.

> **A NOTE ABOUT EMPATHY AND TEXT CHOICE**
>
> In her book *The Empathy Effect*, Dr. Helen Riess describes a phenomenon called *in-group bias*, or a preference toward those who share our physical characteristics. She explains that the roots of this bias stem from our ancestors living in tribes or small groups and depending on people within their group for survival. This in-group legacy becomes a problem when it limits our capacity to experience empathy for people who don't match up to any shared characteristics—the so-called "out-groups." "You may not even realize you have out-grouped whole segments of society, but all of us do" (Riess, 2018). While in-group bias is a truth we must deal with, it doesn't have to limit our students' ability to experience empathy. We can overcome these internal biases by bringing diverse groups of people into the lives of our students through the books we read and by teaching them strategies for practicing empathy. The need to overcome in-group bias is yet another reason why we must diversify our libraries.

Empathy is "when you feel someone's feelings in your own heart" (Mraz & Hertz, 2015). Taking it a step further, empathy is when we share someone's feelings and then react differently because we understand what they experience. The beauty of literacy is that we can marry literature with practicing empathy because reading mirrors and provides context for life and helps us understand the world and one another (Mar & Oatley, 2008). When we read, we share a heart with the characters. We feel the pain of having a best friend move away or being picked last for the kickball team. We experience the joy of baking bread with our grandmother or performing a solo in the recital. Reading and tuning in to the emotions of the characters and to our own reactions can provide emotional context and understanding.

Tucking in Universal Design for Learning (UDL)

The definitive objective for Universal Design for Learning (UDL) is for all students to transform into "expert learners" (CAST Learning Inc. 2018, cast.org). UDL provides educators with a lens of creating and implementing classroom structures in which all students have access and opportunities to the lessons and learning. This resource offers multiple entry points for both educators and learners through the power of stories and conversations. Through the lenses of Identity, Harm and Healing, and Heartwork, we offer students a chance to excel with lessons that offer engagement, representation, and expression. These lessons further align with UDL by leading students to engage in learning with purpose and motivation. When students hear stories about characters they can relate to and learn from, engage in conversations about understanding the characters' experiences and perspectives, and connect or extend their learning through circle conversations, we create moments that invite students to access and engage in learning. This further ensures that our lessons reduce barriers to learning and give student access to education.

All of us need strategies that we can use to support our learners. All of us need read-alouds and mentor texts. This book brings all those needs together, giving you everything you need to support the whole group as well as the personalized needs of your individual learners—plus serving as the perfect mentor text!

The Questions on People's Minds

Before we continue, let's take a few moments to address some people's concerns.

Aren't They Too Young?

For some educators, doing this work in elementary classrooms is challenging because we, or others, question whether students in primary grades are too young for these conversations. Other educators wonder whether school is the place for these conversations to occur. However, researchers have proven that biases and prejudices begin early. We can see from students' behavior that they internalize societal messages about race (The Children's Community School, 2018; Tatum, 1997) and gender (Gender Justice in Early Childhood, 2017). These actions include friendship selection (e.g., choosing only friends who look like them, even in diverse classrooms and schools) and ascribing characteristics to specific identities (e.g., assuming people are more dangerous or less attractive based on skin color; assigning toys, roles, or clothing to a particular gender). Researchers have also found that even at an early age, children struggle with how the dominant culture ascribes goodness or beauty (Clark & Clark, 1947) or gender-appropriateness (Gender Justice in Early Childhood, 2017). These realities support the need to infuse early childhood education with antiracist and anti-bias instruction.

Since 1989, early childhood educator Louise Derman-Sparks has authored texts, individually and with others, that develop and help educators in teaching students to engage in anti-bias ways of being. In her most recent work, she and coauthors Julie Olsen Edwards and Catherine M. Goins state that their ultimate goal is "to support children's full development in our world of great human diversity and to give them the tools to stand up to prejudice, stereotyping, bias, and eventually to institutional isms" (Derman-Sparks, Edwards & Goins, 2020). The essence of Derman-Sparks's early childhood goals for anti-bias education—identity, diversity, justice, and activism—was used by the organization Learning for Justice to develop the social justice standards for Grades K–12.

What If They're (Almost) All White, or If They're (Almost) All BIPOC?
In the poster titled "If the World Was a Village of 100 People," researchers aligned visual images with 2020 statistics to show the diversity across humanity (DeBeaumont et al., 2021). A global economy, along with events such as natural disasters and wars, have increased the movement of populations over the last few decades. As a result, people today are likely to work—physically or virtually—with people who may not look like them. For this reason, cultural competence is a skill employers seek in both BIPOC and White job candidates. The growing diversity in public and suburban schools necessitates that White and BIPOC educators and students develop an appreciation for diversity as well as other SEL competencies and social justice skills needed to be empathetic, inclusive humans who are able to identify and push against oppressive forces. Indeed, the current social climate and state of democracy in the United States reflect a need for citizens who have experienced this type of education.

Don't These Conversations Make White Children Feel Shame and BIPOC Children Feel Inferior?
Feelings of inferiority and shame both center an individual's focus on self. When we center our focus on humanity, there is no reason for either. As creatures who evolved from prehistoric periods, during which our primitive brain needed to quickly read our environment to keep us safe from danger, we—BIPOC and White—are all prone to bias. We—White and BIPOC—are all socialized into ways of being that are affected by ideologies that predate our birth. We—BIPOC and White—are all born into a time period that came after centuries of humane and inhumane acts of commission and omission, which have empowered a few long-standing institutions to bestow rewards and punishment on the masses. These are ALL realities beyond our and our children's control. That means that neither they nor we—White or BIPOC—should feel shame or inferiority when we discover oppression in ourselves or learn truths about history that depict inhumane actions by people with whom we share class, ethnicity, language, nationality, race, or any other identity marker. Neither should we feel superior. We should not feel inferior nor superior—just human.

Shame is actually a barrier to the goals of this work as it can shut down the prefrontal cortex and force a person into fight or flight mode (Arnsten, 2015). Inferiority can have the same effect. This or any other response to stress can result in the opposite of a learning stance. Too frequently, this has been the reality for historically and culturally marginalized students who have suffered school-related trauma. Teachers who engage in culturally responsive and sustaining education, social justice, and anti-bias pedagogies—which all support social-emotional development—prevent and interrupt these types of Adverse Childhood Experiences (ACES) and set young learners of all identities on the path to stronger social-emotional competency. Curating a diverse collection of texts and intentionally drawing from it to design lessons about identity, diversity, justice, and action are effective tools that counter the narratives students learn about themselves and others in society. These tools also develop students' empathy, which is "the antidote to shame" (Brown, 2012) and is necessary to transform classrooms and schools into places of belonging, inclusion, and equity.

Now, let's take some time to think about how we approach this study and how our own identities play a role in our teaching.

LEARNING ABOUT OURSELVES

"It is critical to bear in mind that we cannot engage with our students around these issues when we have not engaged with our own selves. We have to know who we are and where we stand in order to have genuine and meaningful conversations with ourselves and others."
(Mentor & Sealey-Ruiz, 2021)

During the spring and summer preceding the 2020–21 school year, social-media platforms began to fill with educators' calls for "Maslow before Bloom." This was not just a mere suggestion to address students' basic human needs (Maslow) before expecting them to meet educational objectives (Bloom). Aware of the stress and trauma resulting from the pandemic, educators demanded that we focus more on addressing students' social and emotional needs than on making up for their interrupted schooling.

Calls for SEL also resulted from the "racial reckoning" following the murders of Ahmaud Arbery, Breonna Taylor, and George Floyd. How do we do that? Given the lack of curricular connection to realities like this in most educational spaces, many acknowledged the need to implement SEL strategies with care, to avoid subjecting students to the "white supremacy with a hug" that Dena Simmons, educator and founder of LiberatED, has called out for several years (Madda, 2019; Simmons, 2019; Simmons, 2021).

Flash forward to 2023: After a year of book bans riding hand-in-hand with laws against critical race theory and/or historically and culturally marginalized authors or topics, especially those aligned to the LGBTQ+ community, Keisha expands Simmons's description of the concerns about SEL to include not just white supremacy but also "heterosexism with a hug." We should not implement a version of SEL that fails to acknowledge the many ways people identify and express their gender and sexual orientation. Although some people may think this addition unnecessary in primary and intermediate grades, we noted earlier that prejudices, biases, and stereotypes begin to form from an early age. Additionally, research cited by Gender Justice in Early Childhood (2017) suggests transgender and gender-expansive children self-identify as early as their toddler years. Based on this, we must do the self-work to make sure we and our learners develop the ability to be just to community members in and beyond our classrooms who represent the world's various identities.

As we attempt to provide students with support for SEL, we need to **avoid** practices that can inadvertently cause damage and **embrace** practices that celebrate the genius that is present in each student's identities. To do this, we educators must first tend to our own social-emotional learning. We all want to believe we are good people. However, social psychologist and author Dolly Chugh aptly argues that the frailty of humanity makes us, at best, "goodish" (2018), regardless of race, gender identity, or any other social identity marker.

To help us be better than "goodish," this section provides information to help strengthen adult skills, knowledge, and attitudes aligned with SEL and social justice. We recommend reading this section with a journal—physical or virtual—so you can record and review your thoughts, beliefs, and actions throughout and beyond this work. Educators with a growth mindset understand that the learning they do before, during, and after lessons is crucial, not only to their own sense of self-efficacy, but also to their students' learning and understanding. To fully develop the abilities needed to do this work, we need to understand an important aspect of our learning. That aspect is racial literacy.

Racial Literacy as a Mandatory Stance

In her book *The Dreamkeepers: Successful Teachers of African American Children,* Gloria Ladson-Billings expands the concept of pedagogy to include "noninstructional actions, such as smiling at a student or showing disapproval of a student" (2009). She then provides dimensions of culturally relevant teaching that paint a picture of a teacher who demonstrates this type of pedagogy. Such an educator:

- sees herself as an artist and teaching as an art.
- sees himself as part of the community and sees teaching as giving something back to the community; encourages students to do the same.
- believes all students can succeed.
- helps students make connections between their community, national, and global identities.
- sees teaching as "pulling knowledge out"—like mining.

It is important to note that African American students are the focus of this seminal text, which unpacks culturally relevant teaching through research that involved actual teachers. But Black students are not the only beneficiaries of this pedagogy—it is relevant to all students, BIPOC and White as well. This is important to remember when considering the sociopolitical and cultural aspects of the tenets of culturally relevant teaching, as represented in the above characteristics. It also supports the earlier statements about the benefits of such teaching to all learners, whether they are historically and culturally marginalized or centered. This is because these tenets require even students who are traditionally centered to become dexterous in more than their own culture.

Culturally relevant teaching is foundational to both culturally responsive pedagogy (Gay, 2000) and culturally sustaining pedagogy (Paris & Alim, 2017). Both are strengths- or assets-based pedagogies that frame learners as sources of genius. Culturally sustaining pedagogy accentuates the facts that we live in a pluralistic society and that we should nurture and sustain—not extinguish—the rich cultures of BIPOC students through schooling. We can enact each of these pedagogies, and the others required to engage in the heartwork espoused in this book, only through ongoing and intentional development of racial literacy. Racial literacy encompasses several skills. It is "[t]he ability to read, recast, and resolve racially stressful encounters through the competent demonstration of intellectual, behavioral, and emotional skills of decoding and reducing racial stress during racial conflicts" (Stevenson, 2014).

Racial literacy, like all abilities, must be developed. Yolanda Sealey-Ruiz's theory of racial literacy development provides the theoretical framework for the heartwork put forth in this text. Educators must engage in the ongoing work of "excavating" themselves if they are to engage in antiracist and anti-bias teaching and learning with students. When it comes to the level of consciousness needed to do this work well, we cannot overstate the axiom "You cannot teach what you do not know." In areas related to and impacted by identities, we can teach destructive and affirming things intentionally and unintentionally. Therefore, to become racially literate, educators must engage in "a cyclical process of (re)examining perceptions, beliefs, and actions relating to race . . . [and] promote the idea of (de)constructing and (re)building a base for new perceptions founded on open-mindedness and understanding" (Price-Dennis & Sealey-Ruiz, 2021). The components of this process are critical love, critical humility, critical reflection, historical literacy, The Archaeology of Self™, and interruption. Table 2 (below) presents Sealey-Ruiz's definition for each term (Sealey-Ruiz, n.d.) along with some examples of how it relates to SEL and social justice.

Table 2: Racial Literacy Development

Component	Definition	Example (SEL and Social Justice Correlations)
Critical Love	A profound ethical commitment to caring for the communities we live in	Co-creating a community with learners that supports everyone in bringing their authentic selves to the classroom each day (Social awareness, relationship skills, and diversity, justice, and action)
Critical Humility	Remain open to understanding the limits of our own worldviews	Maintaining curiosity about and appreciation of differences (Social awareness, relationship skills, and responsible decision-making and diversity, justice, and action)
Critical Reflection	Think through the various layers of our identities and how our privileged and marginalized statuses affect the work	Seeking feedback from a fellow educator (e.g., coach, administrator, or grade-level colleague) or viewing a recording of a lesson to explore the ways you engage with historically and culturally marginalized students (Self-awareness, self-management, and responsible decision-making and diversity, justice, and action)

Historical Literacy	Develop a rich and contextual awareness of the historical forces that shape the communities in which we work, as well as the society in which we live	Taking the time to learn the systems and organizations in your school's community and how the supports they have or have not provided people have impacted the physical, social, emotional, and psychological safety of students and their families (Social awareness, relationship skills, and responsible decision-making and diversity, justice, and action)
The Archaeology of Self™	Deep excavation and exploration of beliefs, biases, and ideas that shape how we engage in the work	Analyzing the students recommended for intervention to determine if there are racialized patterns, and interrogating yourself to surface any beliefs or biases that might be directing you to implement pedagogies that do not support these learners (Self-awareness, social awareness, and responsible decision-making and identity, diversity, justice, and action)
Interruption	Interrupt racism and inequality at personal and systemic levels	Volunteering to be on data-focused school-level teams (e.g., Intervention and Referral Services Team and Positive Behavioral Interventions and Supports Committee) to support the collective identification of racialized patterns of underserving students through academic and disciplinary practices (Self-awareness, self-management, social awareness, and responsible decision-making and identity, diversity, justice, and action)

(Sealy-Ruiz, n.d.)

The Interconnectedness of SEL Competencies and Social Justice Standards

In December 2020, Karen Niemi, the president and CEO of the Collaborative for Academic, Social and Emotional Learning (CASEL), announced a revision of the "definition and framework to pay close attention to how SEL affirms the identities, strengths and experiences of all children, including those who have been marginalized in our education systems. CASEL has continued to highlight the importance of enhancing the social-emotional competence of all young people and adults, while putting additional emphasis on how we can all learn and work together to create caring and just schools and communities. . . . The updated language pays attention to personal and social identities, cultural competency, and collective action as part of SEL. It also emphasizes the skills, knowledge and mindsets needed to examine prejudices and biases, evaluate social norms and systemic inequities, and promote community well-being" (Niemi, 2020). Because of these changes, the five competencies of SEL and the Social Justice Standards now seamlessly fit together. Table 3 shows the broad connections between the two, and the following pages provide more details.

Table 3: Relationship Between SEL Competencies and Social Justice Standards (SJS)

CASEL		Learning for Justice
SEL Competency*	Equity-Specific Competency	SJS Domain***
Self-Awareness	• Integrate personal and social Identities • Identify personal, cultural, and linguistic assets • Examine prejudices and biases • Recognize beliefs**	Identity
Self-Management	• Set collective goals • Take initiative • Demonstrate collective agency	Action
Social Awareness	• Take others' perspectives • Recognize strengths in others • Show concern for the feelings of others • Identify diverse social norms, including unjust ones • Recognize situational demands and opportunities • Understand the influences of organizations/systems on behavior • Sense of belonging**	Diversity Justice
Relationship Skills	• Co-construction** • Demonstrate cultural competence • Practice teamwork and collaborative problem-solving • Stand up for the rights of others	Diversity Justice Action
Responsible Decision-Making	• Demonstrate curiosity and open-mindedness • Identify solutions for personal and social problems • Learn to make a reasoned judgment after analyzing information, data, facts • Reflect on one's role to promote personal, family, and community well-being • Evaluate personal, interpersonal, community, and institutional impacts • Distributive justice**	Diversity Justice Action

* CASEL's SEL Framework: What Are the Core Competence Areas and Where Are They Promoted?
** CASEL CARES Webinar Series: SEL as a Lever for Equity and Social Justice – Part II: Adult SEL to Support Antiracist Practices
*** Social Justice Standards: The Teaching Tolerance Anti-Bias Framework

The Relationship Between Self-Awareness and Identity

Self-awareness is all about identity. In an article psychologist and educator Beverly Daniel Tatum wrote more than two decades ago, she revealed what makes identity so intricate.

"The concept of identity is a complex one, shaped by individual characteristics, family dynamics, historical factors, and social and political contexts. Who am I? The answer depends in large part on who the world around me says I am. Who do my parents say I am? Who do my peers say I am? What message is reflected back to me in the faces and voices of my teachers, my neighbors, store clerks? What do I learn from the media about myself? How am I represented in the cultural images around me? Or am I missing from the picture altogether?" (Tatum, 2000)

Responding to these questions requires criticality, or the "ability to read texts (including print texts and social contexts) to understand power, authority and anti-oppression" (Muhammad, 2020). On its own, the question "Who am I?" takes a lifetime to figure out and often requires trustworthy and honest friends and therapists to facilitate the learning process. A huge part of the difficulty in answering this question lies in the fact that deep understanding of our self requires awareness of the situationally dependent ways in which the intersection of our social and personal identities may empower or disempower us. We will expand on this later, but it should be clear that surface-level thoughts about self-awareness are not sufficient. Taking the time to answer the questions Tatum presents in the previous paragraph will help us go deeply into the excavation process. Someone who is just beginning to focus on this type of adult learning might find it difficult to respond to all of Tatum's questions. Even a person who has engaged in deep excavation for years would have to take time to reflect on whether previous responses to each question may be different at this moment. But it is worth the time and effort to do this work.

 Take a moment to reflect on and respond to these questions.

- What thoughts do you have after reading Tatum's questions?
- How do these thoughts make you feel?
- Are there any questions you have answered before or could answer now without research (e.g., spending mindful and critical time noticing how media depicts people like you or conversing with a family member or friend)?
- If you don't feel ready to respond to all of Tatum's questions right now, to which questions do you feel you can respond? Underline or highlight those questions. What about the questions you are not prepared to answer at this time? You might write them in your journal along with a plan for how and when you might undertake the inquiry needed to begin answering those questions.

If you are comfortable answering any of the questions, take time now to do this in your journal. If, however, the questions seem too challenging at this stage of your journey, Table 4 presents a social-identity activity with prompts for reflection that may require less research.

 **In your journal, create a copy of Table 4 (below), leaving ample room in the last column to express your thoughts and feelings. Then follow these directions.**

- Under "Your Social Identity," enter the identity you hold for the category in the first column.
- Under "Access/Barriers," note whether that identity provides access or barriers to opportunities and privileges.
- Under "Thoughts/Feelings," write your thinking about that aspect of your identity and your experiences with the accompanying access or barriers you have faced.

Table 4: Social-Identity Activity

Social Identity Category	Your Social Identity	Access/Barriers	Thoughts/Feelings
Ability (mental, physical, neurological)			
Age			
Biological Sex			
Class			
Education Level			
Ethnicity/Culture			
Gender Identity			
Gender Expression			
National Origin/Citizenship			
Race			
Relationship & Family Status			
Religion/Spirituality/Faith			
Sexual Orientation			
Size/Appearance			
Use of English/Other Languages			

Although the Social Identity Activity may be an easier starting point than the questions Tatum put forth, the last two columns may be time-consuming. The third column might even be a challenge that requires reading beyond this text. Reading an article like activist Peggy McIntosh's "White Privilege and Male Privilege: A Personal Account of Coming to See Correspondences Through Work in Women's Studies" (1988) might help inform your thinking.

Navigating Deeper Thoughts and Feelings

As shown in Table 2 (pages 17–18), self-awareness includes knowledge and understanding of prejudices and biases. Digging to this depth is challenging and necessitates a willingness to admit to and contend with self about the truths we uncover. We are more comfortable with admitting positive thoughts we think and positive things we do. We hold so tightly to these that we often struggle to admit, even to ourselves, that we have negative thoughts and feelings regarding some people, and even negative ways we treat some people. Because every person has learned certain ideologies, we all know negative stereotypes about people, including those like us. In addition to those thoughts that we can surface, there are thoughts that exist deep within our psyche—implicit or hidden—that contribute to our biases.

 Look back at Table 4 (page 21) and circle four categories. In your journal, create a copy of Table 5 (below), and then follow these directions.

- Under "Social Identity Category," list each of the four categories you circled.
- Under "Social Identities," list three identities that fall under the category for that row. For example, if you circled "National Origin/Citizenship," you might enter each of the following terms under this column: a. American citizen, b. immigrant, c. undocumented.
- In the next two columns, write three positive and three negative stereotypes for each of those identities. For example, you would write three positive stereotypes of American citizens next to "a" in the third column, and three negative stereotypes about American citizens next to "a" in the fourth column. You would then note stereotypes for immigrants after the letter "b," and so on.

Table 5: Stereotypes

Social Identity Category	Social Identities	Positive Stereotypes	Negative Stereotypes
1.	a. b. c.	a. b. c.	a. b. c.
2.	a. b. c.	a. b. c.	a. b. c.
3.	a. b. c.	a. b. c.	a. b. c.
4.	a. b. c.	a. b. c.	a. b. c.

After completing the table, think about how it felt to acknowledge the positive and negative stereotypes affiliated with different identities. Respond to the prompts below:
- Review each stereotype listed. Are you sure each is listed under the appropriate column—that it is indeed positive or negative? What evidence do you have that this labeling is true?
- Are you aware of the source or origin of any of these stereotypes?
- Which stereotypes represent beliefs you hold about people with the aligned identities? How do you feel about these beliefs?
- Do you think the stereotypes you believe affect your behavior, either positively or negatively, toward people with the aligned identities? What evidence do you have of this?

Keep in mind that it is highly probable that some of your responses to these questions may be incomplete or even untrue. As Chugh writes, "All of us have blind spots. In fact, if you find yourself thinking or saying, 'I don't think I have any blind spots,' then that is your blind spot" (2018). This means it is possible there are stereotypes we are unaware of knowing and believing, that we are possibly avoiding, hurting, favoring, or embracing some people because of unconscious beliefs. Remember that students' racialized and gendered socialization is observable at young ages. The ideologies of oppression, or *smog*, as Tatum calls it, exists, and we learn these ideologies with or without explicit instruction (Tatum, 1997; Husband, 2011; Harro, 2018). Therefore, we are affected by the smog whether or not we can identify it in and around us. Excavation specific to this area is vital as we need to surface how the oppressions in our world impact us to uncover the beliefs that guide our actions.

In her seminal text on the Historically Responsive Literacy Framework, Gholdy Muhammad writes, ". . . pedagogy must be viewed as both an art (imagination and creativity) and a science (theory, strategies, and methods of instruction). This approach calls for teachers to first unpack and make sense of their own histories and identities, which includes the ways they have used language and literacy practices in their own lives. In doing so, they must also unpack their own biases, assumptions, racisms, and other oppressive thoughts they have come to believe about people of color or other people whom others have marginalized" (Muhammad, 2020). It is important to note that the "imagination and creativity" Muhammad mentions are as affected by internal and external ideologies as the "theory, strategies, and methods of instruction" one selects. For these reasons, the *unpacking*, or self-excavation, is crucial. As put forth by Sealey-Ruiz in The Archaeology of Self™ (2021), we must maintain a stance of critical humility, believing there may always be more that we need to surface about ourselves. This will push us to continually interrogate our thinking and the beliefs that drive our actions. The Implicit Association Test (Project Implicit, n.d.) and the Implicit Bias Module Series (Kirwan Institute for the Study of Race and Ethnicity, 2018) provide opportunities to learn more about implicit bias and yourself.

The Relationship Between Self-Management and Action

In a 2017 TED Talk that expounds on his research into racial literacy, psychologist Howard C. Stevenson shares a recording of "the talk"—an actual conversation he had with his younger son, Julian. We recommend viewing "How to Resolve Racially Stressful Situations" (2017) to see a demonstration of Stevenson's racial literacy—the ways he assesses both his and his 8-year-old son's racial literacy and the ways he supports his son's racial-literacy development. He provides details that reveal his deep understanding of the ways stress affected his body during their conversation about the murder of Trayvon Martin and the acquittal of George Zimmerman. As Stevenson narrates his story, we can see how he works to not become dysregulated. To this talk, we can overlay Sealey-Ruiz's theory of racial literacy development (2021).

- **Critical love** – Stevenson made space for this important conversation with his son because he loves Julian and knows the emotional, mental, and physical safety of his son depends on his efforts to foster and nurture Julian's racial-literacy development. He makes sure to convey his love to his son verbally through remarks that provide a psychologically safe climate of belonging and culture of dignity. This encourages his son to share an incident of racial bias that he experienced at a pool and later challenge a perceived misunderstanding to ensure Stevenson understands that surviving a racialized act is most important.

- **Critical humility** – As a Black man, Stevenson is not only empathetic to his son's responses to this type of injustice but also has experienced the same types of reading of the world. Nevertheless, he refrains from inserting himself into his son's processing of the events. Instead, he speaks to validate and expand on his son's thoughts and feelings. Stevenson, a psychologist who has studied racial literacy for years, notes his own awkwardness at points in the conversation. This reflects his positioning of himself as a learner.

- **Critical reflection** – Stevenson's narration clearly shows that he is reflecting in the moment with his son and in the moment with his audience. Both demonstrate his ongoing practice.

- **Historical literacy** – In and beyond his conversation with his son, Stevenson grounds the talk in societal realities. He uses his son's processing of the 2013 report on the outcome of the trial against Trayvon Martin's murderer as a teachable moment.

- **The Archaeology of Self** – From the way Stevenson shares how he has unpacked his parents' different approaches to racism and acts of racialized prejudice to the way he reveals the visible and invisible processing he does during his conversation with his son, it is clear he continuously excavates himself. He mines the thoughts, feelings, and actions that overlay his experiences with himself, with others, and with the truths in the world. This excavating process helps Stevenson uncover the complexities within himself and improve his ways of being in the world.

- **Interruption** – The very act of developing racial literacy is an interruption. We posit that Stevenson's engagement in his own racial-literacy development was the catalyst to and is the sustenance for the research he executes in this area of his life, both personally and professionally.

Through the above analysis, we see the actions Stevenson took, consciously and unconsciously, to manage his emotions during the talk with his son. He used his skills in self-awareness to identify the emotions he felt. He then noted the places in his body that reacted to the rising stress. He supported this regulation of self by remaining mindful, which slowed and mitigated the evolutionary process of freeze-flight-fight. Stevenson's management of himself prevented his reptilian brain, or amygdala, from pushing his body into this freeze-flight-fight reaction. As a result, he could remain physically and mentally present to engage with his son in the difficult conversation. He maintained an active listening stance and a calm tone. He followed his son's lead and worked with him to rehearse their safest path if they were ever in a racialized and potentially violent situation.

 Think about how this connects to the heartwork we suggest in this book. Respond to the following questions in your journal. Be sure to include the emotions you feel as you reflect on each.

1. Have you ever heard a young child say any of the following?
    a. "Your skin looks like poop."
    b. "Why is that lady wearing that scarf over her face?"
    c. "You can't have two moms."
    d. "Girls can't play with trucks."

2. Have you ever said, or heard a colleague say, any of the following?
    a. "That name is too hard. Can I call you ___?"
    b. "Why do we have to find a place for them to pray?"
    c. "That's not a family."
    d. "Boys will be boys."

3. Do you have the courage to interrupt a child or an adult who makes any of these statements? If you are unsure or feel you do not, what would you need to find the courage to do so?

It is important to note the statements made by a young student are vocalizations of the child's attempts to understand the world. These are evidence of the smog (Tatum, 1997). We included these as well as adult statements to help you process them through the self-management skills needed to respond to such moments that may arise with students and/or adults. Taking the time to practice reading, recasting, and resolving each of these situations prepares you to respond in a mindful way when the actual moments arise. Reflecting on the moments after the fact, as Stevenson's example shows, helps you hone your skills so you are more equipped to respond to these situations on subsequent occasions.

The Relationship Between Social Awareness and Diversity and Justice

How do you perceive difference? In an essay written more than 20 years ago, Victoria Purcell-Gates stated:

". . . whether we interpret differences among children—or adults—as deficit or difference depends primarily on our preconceptions, attitudes toward, and stereotypes we hold toward the individual children's communities and cultures. If the child's family is poor, his parents undereducated, his dialect nonstandard, then we are much more likely to interpret experiential difference as a deficit in the child, in the parents, in the home, in the sociocultural community within which this child has grown up. And when we do this, we play God, conferring or denying educational opportunity to individual, socioculturally different, children. And we do not have the right to do this" (Purcell-Gates, 2002).

Too frequently, racial, class, and/or linguistic oppression result in patterns such as those described by Purcell-Gates. This is why we must continually engage in self-excavation and wrestle against those places within ourselves where oppressive beliefs dwell. Uncontested, internalized oppression seeps out through our practice in ways that "other" our learners and deny them the dignity they deserve. Our calls for "Maslow before Bloom" tend to focus more on the Maslowian levels of physiological and safety needs and not on love and belonging, esteem, and self-actualization. But social scientist Matthew Lieberman stated that mammals—which is what we are—enter this world dependent and need others to survive (Lieberman, 2014). He shared brain images that prove our brains register physical and social pain in the same way. Pain medication lessens the effects of both types of pain.

Based on this research, we know that our efforts to both interrogate and mitigate the negative impact of our biases and prejudices are crucial. If we do not take these actions, we might implement a pedagogy that "others" students who hold identities that have been historically and culturally marginalized. Following the logic in Bloom's hierarchy, these types of unintentional and intentional behaviors result in actions that do not raise these students' esteem and fulfill their cognitive needs. If they are to thrive, every one of our students needs to feel they belong and have worth in the fullness of any identities they hold. Feeling a sense of belonging means each student, regardless of identities, feels "appreciated, validated, accepted, and treated fairly within an environment (e.g., school, classroom, or work)" (Cobb & Krownapple, 2019). The creators of this definition of belonging go on to define *dignity* as "the innate, equal worth of each human being simply because that person is human . . . our common heritage and birthright as human beings."

Following the maxim that "you can't pour from an empty cup," we cannot teach social awareness if we are not aware of society's impact on ourselves. The critical love and critical humility needed to empathize with learners who may be different from our own self require thinking about other aspects of ourselves that affect how we show up for ourselves and others.

 **Consider and journal responses to the following questions as well as any emotions that arise.**

- How validated do you feel at work? at home?
- How appreciated do you feel at work? at home?
- How accepted do you feel at work? at home?
- How fairly are you treated at work? at home?

These four questions, loosely aligned to the Indicators of Belonging put forth by Cobb and Krownapple (2019), indicate both the extent to which one's dignity is being honored and the extent to which one feels like they belong in each of their environments. Based on your responses, do you feel your dignity is honored at work and in your home? Similarly, do you feel like you belong at work and in your home? If you answered "no" to either of these questions, how does that make you feel? How might you manage those feelings in ways that impact how you show up in the classroom?

Now, change the questions to consider the experiences of belonging and dignity from the perspective of each student in your classroom whom you consider to be like you. Next, using those same four questions, shift to focus on the perspective of each student whom you think holds any identity that is different from your identities.

 **Here are examples of reframed questions:**

- How validated does Julissa feel in our classroom? in the cafeteria? on the playground? at home?
- How appreciated does Kareem feel in our classroom? in the cafeteria? on the playground? at home?
- How accepted does Tai feel in our classroom? in the cafeteria? on the playground? at home?
- How fairly is Miguel treated in our classroom? in the cafeteria? on the playground? at home?

Further questions you may ponder include:
- Is Hana worthy of your love, dignity, and affection simply because she exists? Or does Hana have to earn your love, dignity, and affection? Why?
- How does Zev experience your pedagogy?
- Do you welcome or avoid Alejandro's parents/caregivers? Why?

As you attempt to do this journaling, consider the evidence that exists to support your perspective for each of the responses for each student. Are the supports for your thoughts based on your beliefs, or do you have objective evidence? Applying the skills you have been honing through journaling, are there any truths you may not be able to see yet because you are still learning to excavate and mitigate your prejudices, biases, and beliefs? Consider the systems that operate in your classroom/school and how they may affect historically and culturally marginalized students. Are there any gaps between what you think you understand about these systems and how these systems affect the ways in which marginalized students are taught? What could be the unintended effects of those gaps? Your responses to these questions reveal the extent to which the classroom and school in which your students are learning are just. While the diversity of our classrooms and schools is often, though not always, beyond our control, identifying unjust practices and taking on the responsibilities to interrupt them is within our power.

To best teach lessons like those aligned to the lenses we put forth in this book, educators should learn more about the community in which they teach as well as the national and global society. One way to do this is to expand our historical literacy by reading texts about histories too often excluded from our educational experiences. Additional activities that can support this learning include conducting home visits at least once each year (these can be virtual family visits, pending social-distancing restrictions) and participating in community activities your students and their families enjoy. Maintaining a learning stance by engaging with curiosity interrupts the evolutionary tendency to become fearful of the unknowns that could trigger a freeze-flight-fight response. Maintaining a learning stance increases racial literacy and strengthens our capacity to execute the pedagogies needed for heartwork.

The Link Between Relationship Skills and Diversity, Justice, and Action
"Relationships are the heart of equity; belonging is the beat and rhythm that shows its vitality; and dignity is the blood that enlivens it." (Cobb & Krownapple, 2019).

Relationship skills best demonstrate that the competencies of SEL are interconnected and interdependent. Human connection requires each person to be self-aware, to manage their "self," to be socially aware, and to make decisions responsibly. To best connect with a student, an educator needs to know their self and ascribe worth to the student. This means we cannot be ability-evasive, color-evasive, culture-evasive, or gender-evasive. As described earlier, we have to acknowledge each and every aspect of the student's identities and view each as an asset that contributes to the genius the student holds. Diversity exists in most of our classrooms. In all our classrooms, relationships require students to feel included. According to Cobb and Krownapple, "[i]nclusion is engagement within a community where the equal worth and inherent dignity of each person is honored. An inclusive community promotes and sustains a sense of belonging; it affirms the talents, beliefs, backgrounds, and ways of living of its members" (2019).

To be an engaged learner, a student must be able to safely show up as their full, authentic self and take risks. Students do not leave their culture outside the classroom. Author and educator Sonia Nieto characterizes culture as "dynamic; multifaceted; embedded in context; influenced by social, economic, and political factors; created and socially constructed; learned; and dialectical" (1999). Therefore, a classroom's culture cannot be one of dignity unless we ascribe worth to all of the cultures that enter the room with our students. A classroom environment that supports this must be psychologically safe to reward vulnerability. Vulnerability is "the birthplace of love, belonging, joy, courage, empathy, and creativity. It is the source of hope, empathy, accountability, and authenticity" (Brown, 2015). Vulnerability allows learners to attain the higher levels of Bloom's taxonomy—analyzing, evaluating, and creating. Table 6, which is adapted from a list of vulnerable behaviors generated by Leader Factor (n.d.), lists many of the learning behaviors that are enabled by a psychologically safe environment. As stated above, an environment that does not provide a student with belonging does not provide that student with the climate and culture needed to reach the evaluating and creating levels of cognition.

Table 6: Acts of Vulnerability

Admitting a mistake	Saying "I don't know"
Asking a question	Saying "no"
Asking for help	Sharing an alternate point of view
Challenging the status quo	Sharing an idea
Disagreeing	Sharing something personal
Doing something you're not good at…yet	Sharing your emotions
Giving feedback	Trying something new

(Adapted from Leader Factor, n.d.)

Cobb and Krownapple define *climate* as "the feel of an environment" and go on to add, "Do people feel like they belong? Can they call their environment their own? Or do they feel alienated?" (2019). They define *access* as "the ability to have opportunities equal to those of other people." Keisha recalls visiting a carceral, or prison-like, kindergarten classroom in which all the Black and Brown boys were not seated at the tables with the other learners but were at desks on the periphery of the room. These boys of color had to earn their way back to the community of learners. How much do you think these boys of color, relegated to the periphery of the classroom, felt like they belonged? How much dignity could these boys feel? How much could these boys trust the teacher and instructional aide in the class? How much psychological safety could these boys experience? How just was this class?

Consider whether these boys of color felt as though they could safely take the risks learning requires. Full engagement in the classroom demands that students not simply be in the room but be considered an integral part of the learning community. Students should not have to earn this position; it should be their right as members of the classroom. For this to become the boys' reality, their teacher would not only have to unpack the biases she holds regarding boys of color but also acknowledge all the identities each boy holds to highlight the strengths each brings into the classroom. As a goal of this self-work, the teacher would need to surface and confront her beliefs that led to each boy's banishment and take steps to become a teacher who deserves the trust of each student. Doing so would mean holding herself accountable—and possibly enlisting the help of the instructional aide or a coach as an accountability partner—for the work needed to develop and maintain a classroom environment in which each learner experiences psychological safety.

As we've mentioned earlier, the characteristics of social-emotional learning are interdependent. To successfully demonstrate relationship skills, one needs to also be self- and socially aware, manage their self, and make responsible decisions. At its simplest, this requires:
- knowing, examining, and mitigating one's triggers (which are impacted by prejudices and biases);
- "demonstrating empathy and compassion" (CASEL, 2020) to another regardless of differences; and
- realizing one's own influence on another in a relationship.

These capacities are required to be culturally competent—an ability needed to be in a relationship with another. Due to the interconnectedness across characteristics, teachers should view challenges in developing healthy relationships with students as evidence of learning they have yet to master. They should work to determine the relationship skills they need to develop, along with other SEL characteristics they might need to strengthen first. Relationship skills are also strengthened by developing the components in Sealey-Ruiz's Racial Literacy Development theory: critical love, critical humility, critical reflection, historical literacy, the Archaeology of Self, and interruption (see page 17).

The Relationship Between Responsible Decision-Making and Diversity, Justice, and Action
"We do not really see through our eyes or hear through our ears, but through our beliefs. To put our beliefs on hold is to cease to exist as ourselves for a moment—and that is not easy. It is painful as well, because it means turning yourself inside out, giving up your own sense of who you are, and being willing to see yourself in the unflattering light of another's angry gaze. It is not easy, but it is the only way to learn what it might feel like to be someone else and the only way to start the dialogue" (Delpit, 2006).

Similar to relationship skills, responsible decision-making draws on other SEL competencies and is strengthened by racial literacy development. A person who is able "to make caring and constructive choices about personal behavior and social interactions across diverse situations" (CASEL, 2020) has to understand their positionality, or the ways their historically and/or culturally marginalized identities intersect and affect their decision-making and those impacted by their decisions. This necessitates a complicated and challenging excavation of self- and social awareness that Lisa Delpit's words help explain. This Archaeology of Self forces each person to unearth the ways they show up and the why behind those ways by making the self an object of deep, ongoing study.

Our natural inclination is to interpret every situation through our own lens. We hold academic, behavioral, cultural, gendered, linguistic, and physical expectations for others based on our ways of being. We read others' academic, behavioral, cultural, gendered, linguistic, and physical performances through our ways of being. If we have not interrogated these truths, we can either miss or inflate the data we glean from others' ways of being. Whether under- or overvalued, the error negatively impacts the decisions we make and our enactment of educational justice. In the classroom, this can lead to prison-like discipline practices, like those Keisha observed in the kindergarten classroom described earlier. Biased or prejudiced readings of others can also result in pedagogical practices and curricular choices that are ableist, heteronormative, racially intolerant, religion intolerant, and/or xenophobic.

For example, Keisha identifies as a Black, fat, English-speaking, cisgender, heterosexual, multiple-degreed, female American citizen. As such, she has to remain curious about the stories of others (e.g., students, family and community members, and colleagues) whose ways of being may not be like hers. She also must consider how differences between her and others affect her decisions as well as how those decisions affect others. Below are examples of culturally responsive decisions Keisha made as a classroom teacher.

- Integrated students' and families' funds of knowledge and ways of being into the taught curriculum whenever possible.
- Took the time to know parents and welcomed them into the classroom to share aspects of their culture.
- Sought out texts, realia, and other ways to represent students and their homes in the classroom.
- Interrupted gendered expectations and teasing in students' play.
- Co-created classroom expectations with students.
- Used her limited, conversational Spanish as much as possible with parents who depended on their children to interpret, and sought interpreters for oral and written communication as often as possible.
- Acknowledged the unease she felt with a student who did not make eye contact, accepted that she would need to unlearn eye contact as the expected behavior when talking with someone, and relearned averted eyes as a behavior to expect from some students (and adults) based on their cultural ways of being.

 **There are many culturally responsive decisions a classroom teacher can make. Think of decisions you have made as a teacher. Then, respond to the questions below and reflect on the reason for each decision you have made.**

- What were your teachers' expectations of how students should perform in each of the following categories: academic, behavioral, cultural, gendered, linguistic, and physical?
- Which of these aligned with the expectations of the adults at your home? Which did not align? How did you feel about expectations that did not align? How were you treated by the teacher? Other adults? Your classmates?
- Were there any students for whom there appeared to be a mismatch between an expectation and how the student performed? If so, what do you recall about the way the student(s) were treated by the teacher? Other adults? Your classmates? You?

- How have expectations that aligned with your home informed your own classroom rules? How have expectations that did not align informed your classroom rules?
- What are your expectations of the ways students should perform in each of the following categories: academic, behavioral, cultural, gendered, linguistic, and physical?
- Are there any students for whom there appears to be a mismatch between an expectation and how the student performs? If so, what do you notice about the way the student(s) are treated by you? Other adults? Their classmates?
- For each student whose performance suggests there is alignment between your expectations and those of their adults at home, what messages have you "read" about their family? For each student whose performance suggests there is no alignment between your expectations and those of their adults at home, what messages have you "read" about their family?
- How have you unearthed each of your students' ways of being? How are the cultures of each of your students reflected in the texts, realia, and other resources and materials you use for instruction? How are they reflected in the materials that are in your room but not used for instruction?
- Have you conducted a home visit, home survey, and/or interview with each family? If so, how frequently?
- Have you administered a student survey and/or interview? If so, how frequently?

These questions are by no means exhaustive. Additionally, your answers to these may not be the same from year to year, even if you remain in the same school and the same classroom. In any given year, however, your answers to these and other questions are reflected in the ways you manage your classroom, design your lessons, engage parents, and distribute resources (including 1:1 time with you). Each action involves multiple decisions. As you engage in the self-work to increase just practices in your classroom, the work you do will have a ripple effect: Critical love will compel you to advocate for just practices to increase for the students beyond your room.

Continuing "The Work"

As this section concludes, we hope it is clear that self-work doesn't end here. It should also be evident that SEL and social justice are interdependent and reciprocal. Skills in one often build from skills in the other, and developing skills in one often strengthens skills in the other. This is especially true when we intentionally connect self-development to racial-literacy development because of the multiple ways we are knowingly or unknowingly impacted by race through racialized systems, such as justice. Understanding this along with how other social constructs—such as class, gender, ethnicity, language, nationality, race, and religion—affect us is lifetime work. We are all products of histories most of us have never been taught. This is why we must do the excavating of ourselves even while we learn the social, including familial, ways we have come to be as we are. As we bring the outcomes of the excavations into our practice, we uncover ways we have grown and ways we still need to grow to impact our students, schools, and communities in a positive way.

LEARNING ABOUT OUR PRACTICES

In this section, you will find a guide to implementing the teaching work within each lesson—from using strategies in whole-class mini-lessons and comprehension conversations to meeting the needs of each student in one-on-one conferences. The lessons are not meant to be followed as scripts, nor do we expect you to do the mini-lesson, conduct the circle, or follow up with conferring conversations with these strategies in mind. Think of the book's lessons as a choose-your-own-adventure exercise. If your intention is to provide students with another strategy in their pocket, you might decide to bring the strategy into a mini-lesson or small group. If your intention is to explore an idea more deeply as a classroom community, you might choose to use the circle portion. To reiterate, this is not a script. It is a toolbox of possibilities with examples and suggestions. Make the teaching and language your own!

Strategies, Steps, and Storytelling

You might equate strategies to the little recipe cards you get in those ready-to-go meals by mail. As you lift the lid, you find all the ingredients and a set of sequenced directions that enable even a novice chef to create a gourmet meal in 20 minutes or less. For readers, strategies act as the recipe for what to notice or ask themselves. Each mini-lesson provides a strategy that teaches readers one way they can expand how they think about books, easy-to-follow steps to make the strategy tangible and clear, and places to pause in the book where teachers can model their thinking process and how it helps them as a reader.

The Places to Pause sections in our mini-lessons are the "I do" teacher think-aloud work of gradual-release teaching. These sections offer examples of possible think-alouds that will bring the strategy to life. Of course, these are just examples of how thinking across the steps of a strategy might go. Feel free to change up the suggestions to match them to your own ideas and observations. That said, don't skip the model! Steps are great; but showing students strategies in action is necessary before we can ask them to try out the work.

While we model strategies in front of our students, it is easy to fall into the trap of asking them for their "help" through the process. Questioning as we model the strategies may seem like a good way to keep our young readers engaged. What often happens, however, is that the back-and-forth questioning makes it hard for students to follow the process, and so they don't see a smooth and clear example of a strategy in action.

Tips on Effective Strategy Instruction

Strategy instruction and modeling work can be used inside many different literacy components. We might tuck strategies into our interactive read-alouds, make them the star of the show in whole-group mini-lessons, or bring them into targeted small-group reading instruction or individual conferences. No matter where they turn up in your teaching, our Top 10 Tips for Strategy Instruction can help lift the level of your strategy work.

TOP 10 TIPS FOR STRATEGY INSTRUCTION

1. Name the strategy and its purpose before you begin modeling.

2. Break down what you're doing into a how-to process with steps.

3. Begin each step with a verb to make sure it is actionable.

4. Intentionally add pauses within your think-alouds to demonstrate that all readers need thinking time.

5. Refer to parts of the book throughout your modeling to show how your thinking grows from the strategy and the book.

6. During modeling, help children focus on YOUR process by avoiding questions and doing all of the talking.

7. Be clear with the steps by using phrases such as "First, I . . . ," "Next, I . . . ," and "Last, I . . ." or lifting your fingers as you teach each step.

8. When thinking aloud, use language such as "Maybe" or "One possibility" to model that there are many ways to answer.

9. Write the strategies on charts so children can refer to them as needed during their independent reading.

10. Be flexible by allowing children to change up the strategy. The goal is thinking, rather than a perfect match to your step.

Balancing Steps and Story

Clear and explicit strategy instruction can provide students with a pathway to success (Serravallo, 2010, 2015; Goldberg, 2016; Hattie, 2018). However, finding the right balance between clarity and a human touch can be challenging. Reading is a personal experience, so we must be careful not to turn our thinking into a set of robotic steps that feels too much like reciting that recipe card rather than teaching. You can avoid the robot-teacher act by genuinely pausing to consider the thoughts that go through your mind and referring to those little bits of the page and picture that brought you to a realization. The best modeling sounds like storytelling our process with a smile.

Another goal for our strategy work is to ensure that our process is transferable and replicable. That leaves us to plan our instruction with an intentional mix of a clearly named strategy in transferable language, its purpose, steps that offer a process for how students might put that strategy into practice, and a bit of modeling that helps them see our steps in action through storytelling our internal thinking.

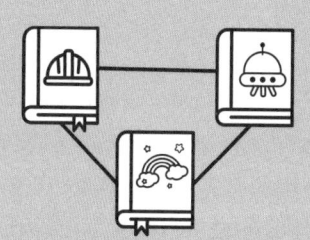

STRATEGIES THAT WORK IN ANY BOOK

To help students understand that strategies can be transferred from book to book, take book-specific language out of the steps and replace that language with general literacy terms. For example:

Instead of: *Think about how the puppy is feeling right now after the little boy yelled at him.*

Try this: *Think about what just happened to the character. Look at his face. Ask yourself, "How might he feel right now?"*

General and transferable language describes what the reader does without referencing the book.

Steps start with action words.

 Harm and Healing

Strategy: Readers look for problems by finding moments when characters' feelings change to upset feelings.

As You Read . . .
- Notice when the character's feelings change to sad, mad, embarrassed, or frustrated.
- Think about what happened right before that change.
- Ask: *What caused this feeling? Is there a new problem for the character?*

Read-Alouds With Heart: Grades 3–5

Classroom Close-Up: Mini-Lesson

For this Classroom Close-Up, we provide an example of strategy work in action during a whole-class mini-lesson. Note: We do not save strategies for mini-lessons alone. We offer strategies as entry points to trying skills during mini-lessons, small-group instruction, conferences, and countless other classroom experiences. Strategies are simply pathways to try out a chosen skill or goal. In this lesson, you'll notice Dana does a lot of the talking. That is because in a mini-lesson, the intention is to model a strategy clearly without any back-and-forth questioning that can distract students from smoothly seeing the steps in action. After modeling, we offer students an opportunity to try that strategy out with a quick turn-and-talk. The lesson takes no more than 10 minutes—a quick in and out to highlight one way of thinking about books.

This lesson features a group of fourth graders exploring Identity and Diversity work through the book *The Journey*, by Francesca Sanna (see page 93).

As Dana heads to the comfy chair at the corner of the classroom library, the fourth graders settle themselves into beanbag chairs, atop milk crates, and on a large square of carpet. With the book on Dana's lap and the students eager to get back into the story, they're ready to begin.

Dana: Good afternoon, Readers! As a community, we've been exploring how our identities shape us and our characters. In making our own identity webs, we've learned so much about each member of our class and found connection with one another. Now, let's consider how we can pay attention to the identities of our characters to understand them and their choices more clearly. One way we can bring identity study into our reading work is by considering how parts of a person's identity can play a role in their actions. When I am studying this connection between identity and actions, I take myself through a series of steps: First, I zoom in on one character and a decision they made. Then, I think about the identities I've connected to the character by listing some of those identities on a web or in my notebook. Finally, I consider how their identities may tie to the choices they made, asking: *How might being ___ make this person want/do ___?* I'm going to try this thinking with the mother in *The Journey*. First, I'll zoom in to one of the mom's decisions. One big decision she made was choosing to leave her home with her children. Now, I'll list some of the identities of the mother character. First up, she's a mom. She's also a woman, a widow, a survivor of war, and a friend.

As Dana lists different aspects of the mom's identity, she jots them on a web on chart paper.

Dana: Okay, now let me think about how these parts of the character might connect to her decision to escape. *(Dana points to the word* mom *on the web.)* Being a mom in the midst of war, especially one that caused her to lose her husband *(points to the word* widow*)*, she would probably do anything possible to protect her children. Hmm. When I think about her decision to leave, I think the need to protect caused her to want to get her children to a safer place, even though it meant going on a scary journey and leaving people she loved and her home behind.

(continued)

Did you see how I did that? I started with focusing on a person and her decision. Then, I took some time to think about all the identities they carry and how parts of who they are influence their choices. Now let's all give it a try with some of our own books.

Dana transitions from modeling to inviting students to engage. She closes *The Journey* and invites students to think about one of their choice books.

Dana: Right now, put a book that you're reading or have recently read front and center in your mind. Think about some of the decisions that a character made. Focus on one that you feel was important to the story. Once you have a character and have chosen one of their decisions, give me a thumbs-up so I know.

Dana gives students a moment of thinking time and resumes when most students have their thumbs up in the air.

Dana: Okay, now think about the identities of your character. For now, just list them across your fingers. *(Dana pauses again to allow students some time to think.)* Great! Now, think about how their identity might connect to their decision. How might a part of who they are explain what they did? Thumbs up when you have something.

When the area is full of students with their thumbs high in the air, Dana prompts students to turn and talk. Chatter fills the room. Students share their ideas while Dana circulates, listening and coaching for a couple of minutes. Students talk about their characters being girls, kids, having divorced parents, and more, and how this makes characters act or sometimes choose not to act.

After a couple of minutes has passed, Dana calls for students' attention and shares that she has heard so many ways in which characters' identities influenced their choices. She highlights one student who talked about how Ruth, a character in the book *The Leak*, by Kate Reed Petty, was a student reporter, and how that pushed her to tell the story of how the lake was causing so many problems for the fish. In this case, the character's job influenced her decision to make a problem public.

To finish up the lesson, Dana reminds students that this strategy could be used for lots of books.

Dana: Let's remember that our characters, just like us, don't make choices out of nowhere. Our choices are influenced by our experiences and our identities, so if we notice that a character is about to make an important choice, we might pause to consider how who they are plays a role in what they choose to do.

Using Circle Questions and Prompts

After reading a book, we want students to dive into productive, deep conversations about its ideas. Because such dialogue doesn't always happen, we need tools to lean on. One of the best tools we know of to get students to think, contribute, and listen is using "circles."

Circles: What and Why

Circles are a structure people use to come together as a community. We gather students in the form of a circle, pose a question or prompt, and then invite them to contribute their ideas and perspectives to the whole community.

Circles and classroom conversation certainly have overlapping goals; however, the format and the benefits of each remain different. In general, circles are not intended as a back-and-forth exchange. Instead, they provide a space where everyone has an opportunity to voice their idea while others listen. See the similarities and differences between circles and conversations below.

Conversations
- Talk moves back and forth between students as they think of responses
- Students agree or disagree
- Students may try to prove their points are correct or find a better stance

Both
- Students listen to hear other perspectives
- Raising hands isn't necessary

Circles
- Every person is intentionally invited to contribute
- Circle protocol sets clear guidelines and norms
- Students reflect on the different perspectives and ideas shared by the whole group

Using circles for communication and connection is not a new idea. Circles have ancient roots in many indigenous cultures. The circular gathering of people in ceremony, dance, mourning, and celebrations allows us to truly be with one another. To share a heartbeat. When we gather as a circle, we become one unit. Circles do more than provide a space for us to sit. They are a living symbol that provides a message of equality, safety, responsibility to one another, and connectedness (Costello, Wachtel & Wachtel, 2019). There is no leader or follower, and all social hierarchy is left behind as we face one another. The unity created in this configuration is the reason circles are broadly used today in recovery, therapies, prayer groups, and, now, in schools.

As literacy teachers, we have been thinking about how we can use circle practices to enhance our reading and conversational work. We have spent decades dreaming about rich whole-class discussions. We have been striving for such rich whole-class discussions, and yet they often have fallen short of fabulous. The reality in our classrooms—and in the classrooms of many other teachers we've worked with—is that when we are in a whole-group situation, a few students carry the entire conversation. The quieter voices never reach the surface, and the gift of their would-be contributions is lost.

For years, our solution was to utilize turn-and-talk or think-pair-share practices, in which everyone had a partner or two and could share their ideas huddled up in their little groups. This allowed for students to feel more comfortable while also inviting the whole group to try, think, and engage. But it did not allow contributions to reach the whole class community. Many voices never made it beyond their little groups and, as a result, their perspectives did not fully move, inspire, or challenge the community. Don't get us wrong. Turn-and-talk is still and forever will be a favorite technique for engaging students in trying out a strategy or exploring some thinking. But when our goal is to benefit from the collective knowledge present in the room, circles are a better choice to embody that practice.

Building Relationships Before Book Talks

Whether handing over a piece of our writing to peers or simply sharing our thoughts with a group, truly showing up is, in many ways, reminiscent of that horrible nightmare in which we end up at school in our underwear. We can't move too quickly into a space of vulnerability. If we do, students will meet us with resistance that shows up as avoidance, silence, or distraction (Nathanson, 1994).

Expecting someone to open up and share their fears, thoughts, and deepest desires can't happen in the first go-round. As a matter of fact, if that kind of sharing does happen too early, it will surely result in what author and educator Brené Brown calls a *vulnerability hangover* (2012). We've all been there. It feels like the morning-after effect—that stomach-plunging moment when you wake up and remember the conversation with an acquaintance that somehow led you to open up and reveal a deep, dark secret you thought was buried so deep it could never surface, especially not with someone you barely know. Whether due to moments of lowered inhibitions or simply because you felt overly comfortable in the moment, opening up too quickly makes us want to burrow back under the covers and hide forever.

> **GETTING-TO-KNOW-YOU PROMPTS AND QUESTIONS**
> - Do you prefer ___ (e.g., cookies or chips, crayons or markers, sunshine or puddles)?
> - Where would you like to go for a vacation?
> - What do you think of when I say ___ (e.g., green, heart, thunderstorm)?
> - What is your favorite thing to play?
> - What makes you smile?
> - What makes you frown?
> - What scares you?
> - Who or what are you grateful for?

One way to avoid the vulnerability hangover is simply to go slow and start the school year by building trust. In your first circle series, stay safe in the shallow water. Begin building this work through the practices of community building in morning meetings. Focus early circles on simple getting-to-know-you type of questions that feel playful and don't reach too far into deeply emotional topics.

Once we've built a strong classroom community, the reasons for circling may shift. In our mini-lessons, we offer circle questions and prompts that support reading and social comprehension. How you conduct the circles, however, is up to you.

There are a few different ways you can implement circles. In the pages that follow, we'll explore the types of circle and conversational structures we use in our practices and the benefits they offer to literacy learners.

Sequential and Nonsequential Circles

During **sequential circles**, we provide students with a question or prompt to consider. Then, going around the circle, either clockwise or counterclockwise, each student adds his or her contribution to the community. (When we engaged in remote-learning experiences, we conducted these same circles by creating a class list that was visible to all the students and moved up or down the list.) Of course, if students are not ready to contribute, they have the option to pass. But our hope is that we have created such a deep sense of comfort in our circles that students will be willing to take a risk and offer up their ideas. Sometimes a student may pass because he or she needs additional thinking time, so we revisit all the students who have passed at the end of the first go-around. This offers them a second chance to bring their thoughts forward. The benefit of a sequential circle is the comfort that comes with knowing when you're going to be invited to contribute.

Nonsequential circles also invite every student to add their contribution; however, these circles do not suggest any particular order. Students who engage in these experiences might simply listen to one another and step forward to contribute when they are ready and there is a quiet space. When they finish sharing, they step back and leave an opening for another student to join in. The benefit of using a nonsequential circle is that students have the freedom to choose when they add their ideas to the community. Those who may need more time to think can give themselves the space to become inspired in a less conspicuous manner.

An alternate form of nonsequential circles that many students enjoy uses a framework in which the last contributor invites another student to step forward. The contributor may hand a "talking piece" to someone else in the group or invite a new person by name. There is something beautiful about having someone say our name

---

ESTABLISHING NORMS FOR CIRCLES

While we play together and slowly open up, we also need to begin establishing clear norms for our community. Coauthoring norms for circles allows students to feel safe sharing their thinking and is much more powerful than having the teacher name the rules of the circle. We might start by explaining to students why circles will be a part of our class community and introduce some general truths about the need for making circles a safe space. We acknowledge that, at times, teachers may decide to begin by offering examples that can be revised with students. If so, here are some common guidelines that can get you started:

- Speak from the heart.
- Listen with respect.
- Speak with respect.
- Share just enough.
- Stay in the circle.

While starters can be helpful for some as we begin the journey, remember that as community norms, students should have some authorship and ownership, even if only through revision. Whether starting from scratch or revising together, here are some questions to support coauthoring circle norms:

- What would a successful circle look like? Sound like?
- What do I need from myself in the circle?
- What do I need from my circle mates?

and invite us to bring our thoughts to the surface. This invitation lets us know that our thoughts are valued and that they have a place here in the community.

As you can imagine, although they are in different forms, all these structures feel more like a sharing session than a conversation. Our goal in these experiences is to allow every voice to be heard and to collect the thoughts and perspectives of the entire group.

Students reflect on what a classmate shared during a circle.

Before conducting sequential or nonsequential circles, be sure to set expectations for students that would allow for a successful experience. We want them to feel ready and have a clear understanding of the length of responses. Finding the right balance in timing can be tricky because while we want every voice heard, we also must be mindful of time and students' ability to stay focused. These sharing circles may call for just a few words or sentences per person. In our experience, younger students do well with shorter responses or sentence stems.

When gathering into the circle, spend the first few moments restating the established norms, that day's timing or response length goals, and then offer the question followed by a moment of silent thinking time. If you have a particularly deep prompt, you may even allow students to think and jot ideas about the prompt before coming to the circle. Having time to dig deep into their hearts and minds can help students feel confident about their contributions.

Fishbowls

Another type of circle configuration is the **fishbowl**. Imagine a fishbowl. Its walls make it a sturdy container, while the fish inside flit about their domain, full of energy and life. In our classroom version, the students in the inner circle are the focus, much like the fish. This is where the action is—where students share, explore, or look for support. The students in the outer circle, like the wall of the bowl, remain still. They are listeners and learners. Fishbowls allow most of the classroom community to become observers and benefit from a few students being centered.

A fun variation of the fishbowl leaves one empty chair in the inner circle. The empty chair acts as an invitation for outer-circle members to hop into the circle if they feel like they have a contribution that could also be helpful. This slight shift in the structure can add an extra layer of engagement to the circle.

TYPES OF CIRCLES

Sequential Circles
Students add contributions in a clockwise or counterclockwise format.

Nonsequential Circles
Students add contributions as they feel moved to speak.

Fishbowls
A small group of students contributes to the circle while others watch and listen.

Flexible Fishbowl
A small group of students contributes to the circle. There is one open seat for someone outside the circle to add a contribution.

Open Seat

But Sharing Takes Too Long!

Some of you may be reading about these circle experiences and thinking, "That sounds great, but there is no way this will work in my classroom. It will just take too long!" We hear you. Bringing whole-class circles together can take up quite a bit of time. So here are a few suggestions to help you benefit from circle experiences in time frames that work within our already busy days.

ProTip 1: Give clear expectations about the length of the responses. You might limit some whole-group circles to single-word contributions or short responses. If you think the answer to the circle question will be longer, consider using a fishbowl.

ProTip 2: Break up the class into mini circles of between five and seven students per group. After students have some community circle practice, they learn how to navigate the circle experience, and you can have smaller circles all running at the same time. Students may not hear every voice in the community, but they still benefit from hearing a few different perspectives and ideas from classmates.

ProTip 3: Use small-group circles as another way to personalize learning. To differentiate learning, we might choose questions that fit perfectly for small groups of students and run small-group circles during a reading workshop or while other students are engaged in independent reading.

Beyond Circles: Using Prompts for Class Conversations

Sequential and nonsequential circles allow us the gift of every voice. They are beautiful and helpful to our communities in so many ways. They help us learn to listen. They help us slow down and focus on just one thing at a time. They inspire us and bring perspectives to the surface that we might not have considered.

Yet there are times when going around a circle prevents us from getting traction with an idea. Conversations require a back and forth—a pausing, taking in, and readjusting of our own thinking based on the contributions of others. When you seek moments of back and forth, we suggest using the configuration of a circle but offering conversational time for students to grow ideas together, challenge one another, and come to brand-new understandings.

One main difference between conversation circles and more traditional circles is that the goal shifts from collecting voices to using our voices to engage with one another. We begin in a similar fashion—by introducing a question or circle prompt. As students add their contributions, we then invite them to challenge, question, or add on to one another's thoughts. The truth is there isn't a community in existence in which everyone is in constant agreement. This is why we feel that creating a space where students can bring different perspectives to the table and discuss them is vital. And by using the circular shape of our gathering, we remind everyone that the interactions must be done with love and respect.

Circles in Book Clubs

The book club is another space in which we envision circles contributing to the conversation. Initially, it might seem counterintuitive to use circles for book club work. After all, book clubs are all about activity and vibrant cross-communication, and we often try to avoid having students go around the club reading their sticky notes and then hitting awkward silence. But using circles in book clubs will not take away the vibrancy and exchange; instead, it adds a layer that makes for better conversation later because of the listening and reflection that the circle offers first.

When pairing circles with clubs, conversations will take on a new structure. The first step is to have students center one big question that they'd like to consider during their chat. The club members should choose this question before they read the next section. Reading through the lens of that question helps students bring focus and intention to their reading and then later to their club conversations.

Before the club meets, encourage students to prepare a response to the common question and begin their time with a sharing circle. At the next meeting, students begin by circling up and sharing their ideas about the common question. During the circle, they can listen to and notice similar and differing views. Then, after everyone has shared, the club takes a moment to pause and reflect on the shared perspectives.

Once you've listened fully to one another's thoughts and reflected on how other people's ideas might push our own thinking, invite students to close the circle and move into full-spirited conversations filled with questions, add-ons, and disagreements that lift the level of comprehension and enjoyment.

> **COMMON SENTENCE STEMS**
>
> Some of the lessons in this book offer specific sentence stems to scaffold the sharing of ideas. Here are some common sentence stems for readers:
>
> - I think . . .
> - I wonder . . .
> - I see . . .
> - I like . . .
> - At first . . . but then . . .
> - I feel like . . .
> - I think [character] feels . . .
> - I think [character] is . . .

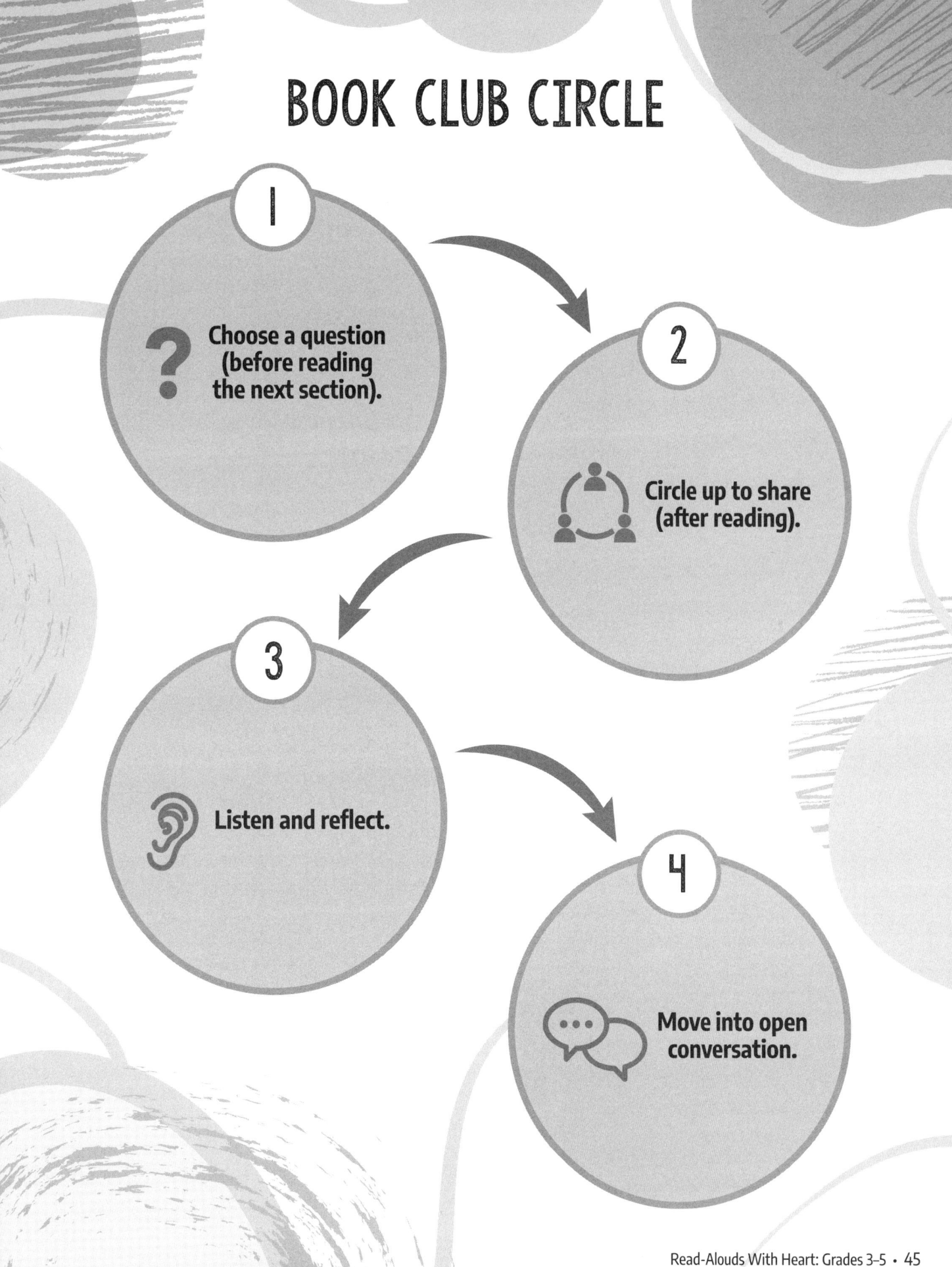

When Conversations Get Tough

We acknowledge that the goal of flowing, respectful, and easy conversation is a lofty one. We know that whenever people gather around and talk about something powerful, passion can lead us into dangerous territory. After all, we've yet to meet someone who doesn't have some sort of holiday family feud story. Consider yourself lucky if your story doesn't end with Aunt Lucy stomping off, Uncle Tony cursing at everyone, and Grandma looking shocked as she desperately tries to wipe the mashed potatoes out of her hair. We can avoid such scenes, however, if we give students the tools to engage in lively yet lovely conversation.

One way to keep these circles safe is to use a facilitator. This person reminds us all of the established norms before we enter conversation and then acts as a guide, ensuring that quieter voices are invited to contribute. The facilitator may also pause the conversation, once again reminding the circle of their agreed-upon norms. This creates space for a mindful moment and may simply add a breathing space that can lower the intensity when emotions become heightened. Facilitators are not meant to lead the conversation, nor do they have more power than anyone else. They are simply there to help ensure that we hear one another's voices and maintain respect within our circle.

We can also provide students with tools to help them navigate conversations both in and out of circle experiences. One of our favorite and most impactful tools is using the word *and* in place of *but*. This simple word switch helps us acknowledge someone else's perspective in conversation while adding another idea that may also be true and important to consider. Let's look at an example. Say this sentence aloud: *I understand what you mean, but I think ___.* This wording sends the message that "I hear you, but my perspective is the right one." Now, try this: *I understand what you mean, and I also think that ___.* Using *and* in place of *but* changes the message to say, "I value your contribution and it deserves to be acknowledged" while also introducing another idea to be considered.

No matter how you choose to bring these conversations forward, we encourage you to embrace disagreement and the challenge of ideas. Sometimes, these conversations will feel uncomfortable, and that is okay. However, if you feel unsure about navigating conversational challenges, try a few of these tools and tips to help you with your journey.

HELPING STUDENTS NAVIGATE CHALLENGING CONVERSATIONS

In her book *Being the Change*, Sara K. Ahmed acknowledges that inviting students into challenging conversations is a must in every classroom and that our learners are going to make mistakes (as are we). This doesn't mean that we should avoid the conversation. Instead, we must teach students how to engage and offer them opportunities to practice. Ahmed writes: "If we want kids to attend to the multiple perspectives around them and listen actively and empathetically, we need to mentor them and show them how" (2018). Check out her book *Being the Change* for invaluable lessons on teaching social comprehension.

How to Grow a Responsive Classroom to Process Difficult Conversations

– Tips from Steve Fiedeldey, International Institute for Restorative Practices (IIRP) Instructor

1. **Plant the seeds of restorative practices early. Feed and nurture deep roots with trust and respect.**
    - Prioritize connection over content.
    - Start with shallow icebreakers, include content-related questions for go-rounds, and eventually lean into more vulnerable, personal questions.
    - Allow student choice in the coursework to demonstrate respect for student autonomy and ownership.

2. **Strengthen the network of connection in the classroom forest.**
    - Just as trees in a forest communicate via an underground network of roots, your classroom will have the same level of interconnectedness when nurtured.
    - Use restorative practices to increase responsibility, equity, and empathy.
    - Lead and model your own vulnerability. Everyone's story matters, and teachers need to share theirs! When you share your story and lead with vulnerability, students will follow. Together, you will share struggles and joys, allowing for greater insights into one another's perspectives.
    - As students share their stories, their roots intertwine around similarities while developing sensitivity to empathy for differences. The strength of this interconnectedness allows for the responsibility and ownership of the class to shift away from the shoulders of the teacher to be shared equally by all learners.

3. **When strong winds and difficult conversations come, trust in the strength of the classroom community.**
    - You are not solely responsible for solving situations or addressing difficult conversations. Lean into the power of the classroom and use the pre-established norms/agreements to remind others of the class's commitments during the healing process.
    - Rely on the interconnectedness of your forest. Whether facilitating a difficult conversation or addressing harm that has occurred, true healing comes when an entire community is involved and all voices have a chance to be heard.
    - TRUST in your students. Trust in the relationships you have developed together, and trust that their voices and unique lived experiences can heal.
    - Hearing from the entire learning community has the greatest potential to effect change.

4. Get comfortable with being uncomfortable.
- You may not have had professional learning, support, or time to prepare prior to a difficult conversation. Do not hesitate to call in others who are further along this learning path to assist in a responsive circle.
- Understanding that a resolution may not be reached is important. Not every difficult conversation ends with a handshake, an understanding of other perspectives, or a hug. Trust in the process. The impact of your collective community may not show itself until weeks or months later, but sometimes we need to give others (and ourselves) the gift of time to grow and change.

Circle Reflection

As you have seen, there's quite a bit of variety in how you can choose to bring circles into your classroom. Regardless of what type of circle you've decided upon, one thing remains the same: Circles should invite reflection. For this reason, we have included an invitation for reflection as a way to close each circle experience. You can do these reflections as another quick circle round, a paired turn-and-talk experience, or simply as a moment of thought.

There are a few common reflection questions that we return to again and again because they get to the heart of why we reflect as a community. Why do we reflect as a community?

- We are one another's teachers and can learn from and be inspired by listening to one another's ideas.
- We find strength in having our ideas affirmed.
- We may see new possibilities or develop new understandings about an alternate point of view when we hear new perspectives.

As the circle closes and the final voices have added their ideas, invite students to stop and think about what they heard from one another during the sharing. As they sit and think, they can use variations of the following questions to help guide their reflection:

- What ideas that were shared stand out to you most?
- What did you hear that taught you something new?
- What new thing can you try?
- What do you now wonder about or want to learn more about?
- What did someone share that made you think, "Me too!"?
- What did someone share that helped you see something in a brand-new way?

Classroom Close-Up: Circles

In this Classroom Close-Up, we look at the structure and flow of conversation within a circle. After sharing a read-aloud, we want to invite students to engage in reflections and discussions that are both deep and meaningful. Circles allow students to come together as a community and share their ideas and perspectives. This is a close-up of a fishbowl-style circle during a lesson with first graders. During their time together, Jigisha shared the story *Alma and How She Got Her Name*, and students engaged in the strategies of identity and connection.

Following the read-aloud, Jigisha opens the circle by asking students to think about their understanding of the character through harm and healing.

Jigisha: Let's think about how Alma felt better from the beginning of the book to the end. What's something that Alma learned that made her happier about her name?

Kate: In the beginning of the story, she looked really sad. And then her dad told her about each of the names she has as part of her name. She learned that each part is from someone in her family, like her grandparents, great-grandparents, and great-aunt. Then she felt special, and by the end of the book she was smiling.

Liam: In the story, Alma was feeling frustrated and upset about her name. She started feeling happier because she knows that she really liked to draw and so did her grandfather José. That connection made her feel special.

Chris: If you look at the pictures on the pages, her smile gets bigger and bigger as you go through the story. *(Chris approaches the front of the class and flips through the pages of the book for his classmates to see.)* It's because she learns what each part of her name means and that she likes the same things as her ancestors.

Miriam: Alma finds something in common with her grandma, like her love for jasmine flowers. Like for me, I am named after my grandma, Mirna, and we are both creative and love baking cupcakes! It makes me happy also when I spend time with my grandma!

Carryover Coaching: Conferring Conversations

We all feel filled up after a powerful class conversation. The community and new ideas grown together are wonderful, and yet for students to achieve continued success, they have to bring their learning and strategies from community time into their independent reading. For true growth, the real goal is transference. In this section, we focus on the Carryover Coaching prompts given for each strategy. Bring these prompts with you into one-on-one conferring conversations and use them to mentor students as they try out new thinking work in their own books.

When to Coach

After teaching a strategy to your whole class and sending students off to cuddle up with their books, you might be tempted to jump right into coaching that particular strategy in your conferences. We sometimes feel the pull of that immediate application, too, and yet we also know that our goal isn't to teach compliance. We want students to apply a strategy as it makes sense in their reading and when it feels like a just-right fit. In other words, the coaching support in each mini-lesson does not need to be an immediate follow-up.

Instead, bring in coaching support as students are ready to apply strategies independently. You might check in by asking lens-based questions to see if or how readers are considering bigger concepts, such as identity or problem/solution. Try some of these prompts and questions as a conversation starter to help you see the kind of coaching a student needs at that time.

Getting to the goal:
- Tell me what you're practicing.
- What are you working on?
- What have you been thinking about?
- What are you trying?

Lens-based starters:
- How have you been thinking about (Identity/Harming & Healing/Heartwork) in your book?
- How are you doing this?
- What have you been paying attention to?
- What has this looked like in your reading?
- Can you show me a place where you've done this?
- Walk me through your thinking.

Dana modeling and conferring with a fifth grader.

In addition to the in-the-moment-decision types of conferences, we may also plan some intentional coaching time to support our young readers. These planned interactions often take the form of coaching conferences and small-group support time. We know that mastery doesn't happen in the space of a five-minute conference or a ten-minute mini-lesson. Time and practice are necessary ingredients for growth, and a bit of coaching can assist along the way. If you've already taught a strategy and want to follow up with some one-on-one coaching or if you feel that a small group of learners may benefit from practicing a strategy, you might pull out our Carryover Coaching prompts for small-group practice or reinforcement coaching.

Acknowledging the Balance

In the few years it has taken to bring this book to life, the literacy world has turned back the clock and reignited the reading wars. And it has gotten ugly, with lots of blame, finger-pointing, and binary thinking. Educators are landing in camps, digging their heels into their own beliefs, and not really thinking about who this impacts the most—the students. It is not our intention to solve the sad truth of where we are in a paragraph or two; however, we do want to take a moment to acknowledge our belief in balance. There should not be camps in this conversation—it's not an OR conversation at all. It's an AND conversation.

Students need instruction in foundational skills. They need explicit instruction and opportunities to engage playfully with phonemic awareness, phonological awareness, phonics, vocabulary, fluency, reading comprehension, oral language, and writing. But we need to teach them that reading is much more than reading the words. Reading is thinking, feeling, learning about the world, wondering, and being inspired. Reading is understanding.

Literacy is a BIG word, and there is a lot to learn. This book touches upon a few parts of this work. There needs to be time and space in the day to honor the other aspects of literacy learning as well. In the end, staying balanced is no easy feat, but we know that to help our readers grow, we have to do more than teach just one thing. Yes, we need to focus on helping them say the words on the page, but our job doesn't end there. We hope that this text serves you in your efforts to support reading comprehension and conversation in your classrooms, and in our hearts, we remain hopeful that educators will find their way back to balance and one another.

Just Enough

It's tough to find the right balance of support during personalized coaching. We want students to be successful. We want them to laugh at the funny parts and shed a tear with the characters in the sad moments. We want them to understand their books. But we can't let our drive to support them lead us astray. It is very easy for us to lead students, especially when we find them hesitant to chat. However, when our pattern is to lead students, multiple problems follow—from sending messages that there is only one right answer to taking away a student's ability to practice. This is something we must avoid. On the flip side, allowing students to just name a strategy may not be enough. So, if we aren't doing the work for them AND we are not leaving them to do it on their own, what does a coaching conversation sound like?

> **LEADING CAN LEAD TO PROBLEMS**
>
> 1. We set up the expectation that students should respond with the idea that is in our mind rather than have a genuine response themselves.
>
> 2. We do all the work, and they know it. Students will pick up on the fact that if they wait a moment or two after you ask a question, you will answer or do the work for them.
>
> 3. Students don't actually practice a skill or strategy at all, so they don't actually grow as a result of our interaction.

During coaching conversations, our role is to nudge. We want to slow down the strategy, breaking it into lean prompts that will assist the reader in real time. Like the strategy's steps, prompts begin with actionable verbs, such as *look, read, find,* or *think*. This gives students a tangible step to try out in the moment.

You may notice that the first few times a student tries out a strategy or way of thinking about a book, there will be more pauses and places for you to coach into their process. As students continue practicing, the thinking we might have been coaching them into will become part of their process. Since our goal is ultimately for students to do this work independently, our prompting should fade and we might instead simply offer encouragement and nonverbal cues that reinforce the student's thinking (Goldberg, 2016).

> **Classroom Close-Up: Conference**
> In this Classroom Close-Up, we look at ways we can use our strategies to support students in their independent reading. This is a snapshot of a conference with a fourth grader. During their time together, Jigisha asked her what she had been working on, listened through asset-based lenses for all the things that she was already doing well, and then used one of the strategies to coach a next step.
>
> A few minutes after the mini-lesson, the students settle in with their independent reading and are already immersed in the stories they hold in their hands. Jigisha walks over to Claire and asks if she can interrupt her reading for a few minutes to chat. Claire looks up with a smile and nods her head. Jigisha pulls up a seat next to her and begins a conversation that dives deeper into the work of reflecting, honoring, and understanding.
>
> **Jigisha:** Looks like you're reading *Number the Stars* and you've taken notes in your notebook. I also see you have sticky notes throughout the pages that show your thinking. That's wonderful! Let's talk about what you're thinking. We've been studying how we can learn about characters by studying how they react when they are treated unfairly, and how certain groups of people are treated unfairly because of their identity. What have you been practicing?
>
> **Claire:** I've been thinking about characters who are treated unfairly because of who they are, like, their identity.
>
> **Jigisha:** Awesome! Can you share some of that thinking with me? Show me an example from the book. How are you taking notice of this in the story?
>
> Claire turns through the pages filled with sticky notes to the chapter she has just finished reading.
>
> **Claire:** In this part of the story, we see that Annemarie and her family are trying to help Ellen. Ellen is Jewish, and at this time in Denmark, some people did not like Jewish people. Annemarie

(continued)

and Ellen are best friends, so Annemarie wants to help because it's not fair how Ellen is being treated. At one point, Annemarie wants to say something back to the guards, but she doesn't.

Jigisha: Oh! It looks like you're using what we have learned about the characters and their identities and making connections to their experiences. You're looking at the actions of the characters, you're paying attention to what they're saying, and you're making connections between what you know about a particular time in history and this story. You do all the things we do in real life to understand who people are and how they might be treated because of that, even in those times when it is unfair.

Claire: Yeah. There was another book I read, the story about Malala, where girls weren't allowed to get an education just because they were girls! And I don't think that's fair, because I can't ever imagine not being able to come to school because of who I am.

Jigisha: Wow! That's such a wonderful connection you made to the biography that you read about Malala. I think you're ready to try out another thing around characters and their actions. One other thing that readers do is try to go beyond looking at the main character's actions and also look at the other characters' actions to help us understand their perspective. You can do that by looking for the words and actions of the other characters as well as the interaction between characters. You shared a bit about the main character, but let's switch to other characters. Pretend to be another character and think about their actions and reactions. Think about their words. Push yourself to see from this character's perspective. Think about this from the character who might be part of the same or a different identity group.

Claire: Okay, I'll try that. I'll also use my sticky notes to help me think about it. It helps me keep track. Sometimes I use different-colored stickies for different notes, like feelings, dialogue, or whatever I am thinking about the book.

Jigisha: Great, that's a wonderful strategy! Let me show you using the story I have here. *(Jigisha opens the book* The Fearless Flights of Hazel Ying Lee, *written by Julie Leung and illustrated by Julie Kwon, a mentor text that the students already know well. She points to the part in the book that shows Hazel feeling upset.)* Remember this part? We read and see that Hazel feels defeated because she's not able to fly the planes to help her country during the war, even though she's an incredible pilot. This was because of her identity—the fact that she was Asian and that she was a woman. Now, I'm going to look at the other characters. We see toward the end of the story how her family feels heartbroken, because after Hazel passed away, the country did not honor her or allow her to be buried in a cemetery that honors pilots during the war, even though she did so much to help. We see her family take action against the unfair treatment by writing a letter to the president. Hmm . . . as I think about this part from all the characters' points of view, I can understand how this unfair treatment impacts all of the characters and their identities. You try.

(continued)

Claire opens her book to look back at the chapter she just read.

Claire: I'm going to think about Ellen's perspective this time.

Jigisha: Great! As you take note of her actions, the things she says, and even her interactions with Annemarie, imagine you are her and how you might react to the unfair treatment.

Claire takes a moment to read over the pages again and jots notes on her sticky notes.

Claire: I see that Ellen is more of a quiet person, but she is the one who is being treated unfairly because she is Jewish. She probably feels lucky to have a friend like Annemarie, but she is probably furious and confused about how she and her family are being treated.

Jigisha: Yes, now you're looking at the actions and words of both characters. That helps you see more about their perspectives. When we think about how the characters are being treated unfairly because of their identity, reflecting on and analyzing Ellen is so helpful to understand the story more deeply. As we read, we can get a stronger understanding of the moments, actions, and reactions of the characters through their experiences.

Beyond the Book

The final section in each mentor text invites your class to take the thinking they've done as a community outside of the book and into real-world practice. Our intention is to bridge the literary world with our world and think about how understanding the experiences of real or imagined people from our books can change the way we live every day.

These invitations vary in form. Some of them feature role-play scenarios that allow students to practice how they might act or react in social situations. Others are circle prompts that move away from talking about text and into talking about life. Some prompts are calls to action that invite students to make positive changes in their own communities, while a few are simple mantras that can help us all with the self-talk that leads us in positive directions.

Literacy, Social Comprehension, and SEL

A truth that we often speak is that our job as educators doesn't end with teaching students how to read. Of course we want our students to be able to decode, accumulate text, and think about the books they read once they leave our classrooms. But even more than that, we want to support students in understanding more than just books. We want them to understand themselves, one another, and the world in which they live. We want them to contribute to the communities that they are a part of today and the communities that they will become a part of tomorrow.

Because our goals tie in to supporting reading, social comprehension, and social and emotional learning, many of the lessons and strategies in this book have been inspired by two of our favorite professional communities: Learning for Justice and the Collaborative for Academic, Social, and Emotional Learning (CASEL). If these two organizations are not already bookmarked as favorites on your browser, we suggest you dive into the amazing tools and resources they offer on their sites and through their professional learning opportunities. The lesson work in this book will reference Learning for Justice's Social Justice Standards and CASEL's five areas of competence.

Reading Aloud and Revisiting Stories

The mentor texts featured in this book are not meant to be one-and-done reading experiences. Introduce a chosen text to students as an engaging read-aloud. During this initial visit, students follow characters through the twists and turns of the plot and pause to react to the characters' experiences and emotions. Choose multiple stopping points along the way to share your own thoughts and invite students to think about the story.

Let's take a moment to explore the two types of read-aloud experiences: **read-aloud** and **interactive read-aloud**. When some of us think about read-aloud time, we imagine students huddled together listening to the teacher read a story straight through without interruption. These community moments offer students an opportunity to hear a book come to life with fluent and expressive reading and to simply enjoy a story together. These types of read-alouds are certainly worthy of our class time. However, read-alouds can also take on an instructional lens. In the interactive read-aloud experience, the reader pauses at chosen points to model some thinking or to invite students to consider new ideas and put some strategies into practice (Fountas & Pinnell, 2001).

There is no right or wrong read-aloud practice when you engage in a first read. Follow your heart and feel free to mix it up. Either way, before diving into explicit strategy work or circle practice, students should first experience the book as a joyful community read. As Maria Walther shares in her wonderful book *The Ramped-Up Read Aloud*, "A read aloud should be a joyful celebration for all. For you, for your students, and indirectly, for the author and illustrator who toiled over each word and every image that lies on and between the covers of the book" (2019).

After the classroom community has enjoyed the story together, that book becomes a mentor text that can be revisited again and again for different purposes. It is during these revisits that you will highlight specific parts to model a **strategy**, invite a **circle** conversation, or tap into a **beyond-the-book** social and emotional learning experience. Each mini-lesson features a preselected section of the book for you to revisit and explicitly teach the strategy. In these moments, we reread a short section of text and model for students how we think through the chosen strategy so we can offer them a clear example of the strategy in action. Think about your revisit decisions as an if-then scenario. If you want to teach a clear strategy for a way readers think about texts, then revisit with a mini-lesson. If you want to offer a space for perspective sharing and benefiting from one another's ideas, then revisit with a circle. And if you want to use the text as a catalyst for some social comprehension work, then revisit with a beyond-the-book lesson.

Classroom Close-Up: Circles

Storytelling is an art form that is integral to humanity. Stories engage us at our core. Well-crafted stories stay with us long after the experience of hearing them and compel us to share them with others—expanding and connecting through spoken or signed language—and allow us to share our individual transactions with the text in a way that creates a communal transaction.

There are times when experiences like these can start with the first page of the story. The community gathers with each member, ready to engage and begin creating deep meaning from just the words and illustrations. There are other times, though, when the background knowledge needed or the emotional management that might be required calls for a circle before the first page is read. In this Classroom Close-Up, we will look at one of these times.

Understanding that two sessions would be optimal based on the length of the text, Keisha prepares two nonsequential go-arounds—one to launch each read-aloud of *The 1619 Project: Born on the Water*, written by Nikole Hannah-Jones and Renee Watson and illustrated by Nikkolas Smith. During the nonsequential go-around that launches the story, Keisha sits at the document camera in the classroom and asks students a simple question: *What brings you joy?*

Intentionally planned, the question serves two purposes:
1. It prepares students to engage with the people centered in the text. Their answers will align with the types of "joy-producers" the text will convey about the people of the Kingdom of Ndongo. This will both call attention to and center the shared humanity, helping the majority American and White students to empathize with indigenous African people living in a time far from their current reality.
2. It connects with the theme of resilience that not only is inferred in the text but also serves as an example for readers of the ways to persevere in the face of difficult and challenging times.

(continued)

As an adult visitor to the classroom community, Keisha responds first to the question to not only position herself as a member joining with the learners in this reading experience, but also to model vulnerability by sharing this information about her out-of-school life. The students (whose names have been changed) quickly engage.

Adam: Take-out food and soccer
Carey: Music
Eddie: Singing and art
Greta: Dance and my mom
Isaac: Going in my hot tub
Karen: Going to new places

During the first of the reading, several students verbally or physically show a connection when joy-producers they shared or jotted down were read from the text of the poems "They Had a Language" and "Their Hands Had a Knowing." The students embrace the humanity of the people in the story. Through that connection, many move from simply viewing the examples of life in Ndongo to walking through the "sliding glass door" into that life (Bishop, 1990), imagining themselves living in that place at that time.

When we read the last page for the day's session, students express audible signs of sadness, and not just in response to being forced out of the story. Those students who are transported to Ndongo do not just feel they are being made to stop viewing a scene in which people are being kidnapped. They feel themselves pulled from their loved ones and their familiar home.

While all of the students have visceral reactions that provide evidence of their ability to empathize, those who imagined themselves experiencing the joys are most affected and verbalize, without prodding, the extent to which they are aggrieved as "Stolen" is read. Whether a viewer of the events in the story or transported into it, each is able to relate to the point of view of the Ndongo people and understand the extent of the harm done against their humanity. This strengthens skills students are developing in the identity, diversity, justice, and action social justice domains.

As is always the case, these types of deep transactions with text are only a hoped-for outcome when the lesson is planned. Thankfully, Keisha and the other adults in the classroom are able to immediately assess the lesson's effectiveness by the time students are asked to pull out their readers notebook and capture their thoughts up to this point in the text, concluding their work for the day and providing more evidence that can be used to revise the plans for the second session.

READ ALOUD

Enjoy the book as a class community. Pause at times to think aloud and invite students' thoughts and reactions.

REVISIT FOR MINI-LESSON

Look back on a small section. Use that section to model your thinking through a strategy.

REVISIT FOR CIRCLE

Share the circle question with students. Reread a portion of the text or the whole story before the circle chat.

REVISIT FOR SEL

Revisit sections of the book that highlight lessons, role-playing, or other social and emotional learning activities.

THE LESSONS PART

"Reading is not walking on the words; it's grasping the soul of them."

– Paulo Freire

We wrote a book focused on mentor texts because we believe the characters, images, and words on the pages of a book can touch our souls and shape the people we become. Books can offer students learning opportunities well beyond skill development and enjoyment. Books hold our humanity, and reading about the lives of real or imagined characters can give students the gift of understanding themselves and one another.

Lesson Page Close Up

Each lesson begins with a mini exploration of the mentor text that includes a genre description, grade-level recommendation, and a summary of the book. You'll also find three lessons—one for each Reading Lens—that offer strategies with places to pause and model your thinking process, questions that can be used for whole-class conversations and circles, and carryover coaching prompts that bring these ways of thinking into small groups and conferring work.

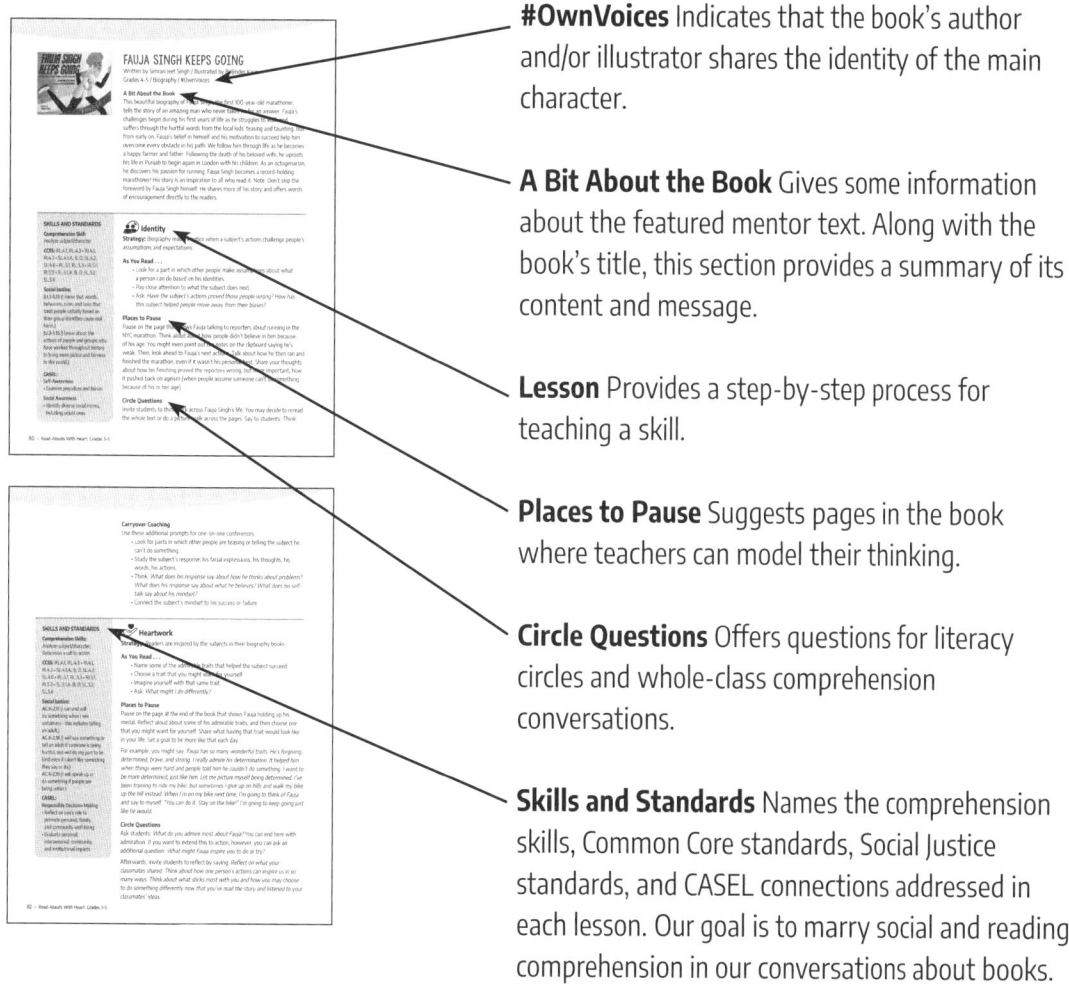

#OwnVoices Indicates that the book's author and/or illustrator shares the identity of the main character.

A Bit About the Book Gives some information about the featured mentor text. Along with the book's title, this section provides a summary of its content and message.

Lesson Provides a step-by-step process for teaching a skill.

Places to Pause Suggests pages in the book where teachers can model their thinking.

Circle Questions Offers questions for literacy circles and whole-class comprehension conversations.

Skills and Standards Names the comprehension skills, Common Core standards, Social Justice standards, and CASEL connections addressed in each lesson. Our goal is to marry social and reading comprehension in our conversations about books.

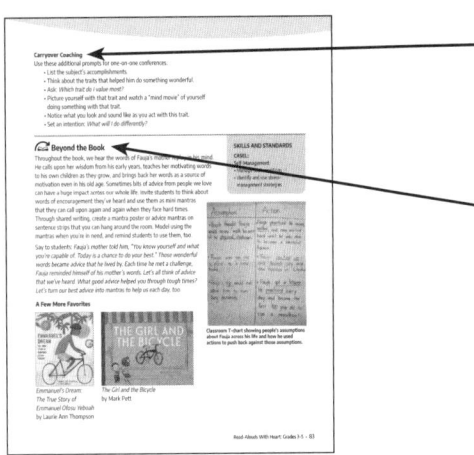

Carryover Coaching Provides general questions and prompts teachers can use to bring the strategy to independent readers in reading conferences.

Beyond the Book Extends the work into intentional SEL study using games, self-regulation strategies, or community projects. Each activity is designed to help students build community and practice social comprehension.

Note: Italicized phrasing and questions offer examples of verbiage and questions you can use in the classroom. Our intention is not to create a script but to share sample language.

We wish we could include all the books we have read and loved and tell all our stories within this text. However, we are limited to page numbers that help make this book a little lighter to carry in our classrooms. At the end of the lesson pages, you will find a few more book recommendations that invite us all to continue deeply exploring the lives of people, identities, homes, and worlds.

Putting Lessons Into Practice

Anything worth deep study deserves more than a one-time visit. We imagine the concepts of Identity, Harm and Healing, and Heartwork are threads that weave across the school year. Each woven lesson provides yet another stitch in the blanket of literacy and social-emotional learning.

The lessons on the following pages are designed to fit within any literacy framework or program. To be clear, this resource is not intended to become a whole program or curriculum. We see this book as a tool to enhance your yearlong study, not replace it. There are countless ways you can bring these stories, conversations, and strategies into your classroom study, and we trust that you will find your own unique approach to incorporate the work. We invite you to consider a few possibilities for adding or swapping out some of the books you are currently using for those in this section.

Here are a few suggested frameworks for choosing lessons:
- Matching skills and standards
- Matching genres
- Connecting to content areas
- Honoring celebrations, identities, and relationships

Matching Skills and Standards

As with most large shifts in education, the adoption of the Common Core State Standards in 2010 was anything but smooth sailing. Dana remembers many a faculty meeting spent sitting around a table with her first-grade teacher colleagues, and everyone scratching their heads trying to figure out what these new standards meant and how they would change the work they were doing with their students. They debated, looked at student samples through the lenses of the standards, and spoke at length about the developmental appropriateness of certain ideas. Coming to their own interpretations of the meaning behind the standards took time and energy. Many struggled with concepts such as text-dependent questions and finding authentic and meaningful ways to bring close reading into a first-grade classroom. It certainly wasn't all fun and games, and many of the practices they tried were abandoned. Yet in the end, the team found value in the way these standards worked as a giant learning progression—laying out a K–12 view of how skills grew with study and practice. In addition, the standards gave more clarity to the importance of focusing on different genres and balancing fiction and nonfiction reading experiences. Most important, the layers of comprehension standards sent the message that literacy learning was about making meaning and not simply about learning letter-sound correspondence and decoding words on the page.

It's been more than a decade since Common Core came into being, and in that time, the lessons we've learned through implementation have led many states to revise or create their own versions of the standards. This is how learning goes—we try something new, we reflect, we celebrate our successes, we learn from our failures, we refine. Today, standards are just one tool to help us plan our literacy lessons. We know there is no magic wand that will accelerate growth, but we can hold up the standards as a way to consider some important frames and skills that will help students explore texts and their ideas about those texts in new and interesting ways.

If your lesson planning is centered around different standards or skills, you can use the book chart online (see page 6 for how to access) to match the standard/skill you are teaching with our books and lessons that address that type of learning. For example, if you need books and lessons that support standard RI.4.3 *(Explain events, procedures, ideas, or concepts in a historical, scientific, or technical text, including what happened and why, based on specific information in the text)*, you can scan the book chart and find texts with lessons that address that standard (see example on the following page).

Title	Author/ Illustrator	Identities represented*	Ideas represented	Genre	Core standards	Identity	Harm and Healing	Heartwork	Awards
Fauja Singh Keeps Going	Simran Jeet Singh / Baljinder Kaur	Race: Asian Ethnicity: Indian Religion: Sikh	Overcoming obstacles; ageism; religious bias	Biography; narrative nonfiction	RL.4.1, RL.4.3, RI.4.1, RI.4.3, SL.4.1.A,B,D, SL.4.2, SL.4.6, RL.5.1, RL.5.3, RI.5.1, RI.5.3, SL.5.1.A,B,D, SL.5.2, SL.5.6	Readers notice when a subject's actions challenge people's assumptions and expectations.	Readers study the subject's/ character's mindset when facing challenges	Readers are inspired by the accomplishments of the subjects in their biography books.	Christopher Award for Young People, 2001–2022 Winner; Notable Books for a Global Society, 1996–2022 Selection; El día de los niños / El día de los libros, 2013–2022 Selection

*Like all of us, the characters and subjects in books carry multiple identities. Our identities go beyond our cultural heritage and races. Identities are also our family roles, our careers, our interests, and so much more. It would be impossible to capture every part of a character's identities in a small chart; therefore, we focus on only a few for each book. The list shown here does not capture a full picture of someone's identity.

Matching Genres

In addition to focusing on skills and standards, many educators organize learning through genre studies. There may be times in the year when we invite students to read primarily biography texts, or we may take a dip into folklore or historical fiction. These genre studies give students the opportunity to explore elements and specific characteristics tied to different text types and broaden the ways they create meaning. When planning for genre studies, you might decide to focus on the genre category on our book chart online. Then, scan and select texts that would support the genre exploration that you and your students are about to engage in.

Connecting to Content Areas

While it is true that the focus of the strategies and circle conversations in this book are connected primarily to literacy, the stories we've chosen may also find their way into content-area teaching. Dana, Keisha, and Jigisha have always found that the most authentic and engaging ways to learn content are through play, curiosity, and storytelling. Bringing picture books into the content areas can ignite interest and invite students to bring their most curious selves into that study. A picture book can be just the tool that you need, whether to introduce a new topic or to connect abstract concepts to real-life experiences and people. Check out the book chart online for matches to people, time periods, and even scientific discoveries that fit with the content you are teaching. These books and lessons may be a way to bring a bit more storytelling and context to subjects you're studying in history and science.

Honoring Celebrations, Identities, and Relationships

Lastly, we'd like to honor that not all learning fits into neat categories, such as reading instruction, math, or science. Sometimes, our learning is inspired by celebrating the wonderful people in our lives and in our world. While we don't need to—nor should we—follow a calendar to bring different cultures into our classroom, books are a wonderful kickoff to honor cultural celebrations, such as Hispanic Heritage Month or Grandparents Day. We do not suggest sorting the identities represented in our highlighted texts into categories, such as Pride Month books, Black History Month books, and so on. We strongly believe that representation of all different identities should be woven across time. However, you might see that one of the titles listed in this book provides an ideal opening into a celebration.

In our role as educators, we have opportunities to dedicate ourselves to transforming our teaching by celebrating this work throughout the year—and not just in a particular month. The stories found within this book offer an invitation and an opportunity to dive deeper into these lessons! If one way to use these texts is as an entry point into a cultural celebration, you can use the identities section of our book chart online to match up the people that you may be honoring with great biographies and books. You may circle back to the same text at another time of the year to offer a lesson through Harm and Healing, and again in another moment, through Heartwork. The flexibility of the lessons found within this section offers educators numerous options and provides students with multiple experiences with one text.

As you move into the lessons on the following pages, we hope you will see the beauty both in the texts and in the conversation and thinking that we invite students to engage in with one another. We hope these conversations in classrooms will help students feel seen, appreciated, and inspired. We hope you will feel that way as well.

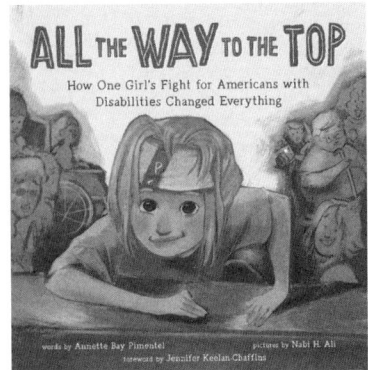

ALL THE WAY TO THE TOP:
How One Girl's Fight for Americans With Disabilities Changed Everything

Written by Annette Bay Pimentel / Illustrated by Nabi H. Ali
Grades 3–4 / Biography

A Bit About the Book
This empowering and riveting true story tells us about the life and activism of Jennifer Keelan. As a child, Jennifer faced several obstacles due to her disability. She experienced hardships in school and with other children her age because she was in a wheelchair. Jennifer overcame both physical and societal boundaries with positivity and courage. With the support of her family, she discovered a community with other disabled people like her. Together, they engaged in activism for equality, even though Jennifer was still a child. Her history-making moment came when she hopped out of her wheelchair to climb the stairs of the U.S. Capitol Building to advocate for laws that would support individuals with disabilities across all spaces. Read through Jennifer's journey of hope, courage, and empowerment. Be sure to read the foreword written by Jennifer Keelan herself!

SKILLS AND STANDARDS

Comprehension Skill:
Analyze subject/character

CCSS: RI.3.2, RI.3.3, RI.3.7, RI.3.8 • SL.3.1, SL.3.4 • RI.4.2, RI.4.3, RI.4.7, RI.4.8 • SL.4.1, SL.4.4

Social Justice:
JU.3-5.14 (I know that life is easier for some people and harder for others based on who they are and where they were born.)

CASEL:
Self-Awareness
- Integrate personal and social identities
- Link feelings, values, and thoughts
- Examine prejudices and biases
- Have a growth mindset
- Develop interests and a sense of purpose

Identity

Strategy: Readers of biographies analyze how the setting impacts the subject's life or experiences.

As You Read . . .
- Pay attention to the setting.
- Think about the subject's identities.
- Ask: *How does this setting affect the actions the subject can take or experiences she can have? How does that connect back to her identity?*

Places to Pause
Pause on the pages in which Jennifer attempts to go to school. Share what you notice about how Jennifer interacts with her surroundings. Think aloud about the connection between Jennifer's wheelchair and her difficulties in entering the school. Share what you notice about Jennifer's reaction and how she continues to persevere in the face of these hurdles.

Circle Questions
Say to students: *We notice that Jennifer is allowed to enter a school but can only join for the afternoons. When she's in the classroom, some of her classmates react by saying, "You'll never be one of us." Share a time when you*

felt excluded or when you saw someone being excluded because of something related to their identity.

Afterwards, invite students to reflect by saying: *Let's think about how Jennifer felt when she was excluded and some of the experiences your classmates shared. Let's hold space for this feeling. Place one hand on your heart and take a deep breath in through your nose. Hold the breath and think about those feelings. Now, gently exhale out. Let's repeat one more time together.*

Carryover Coaching
Use these additional prompts for one-on-one conferences.
- Find sections that show the subject's interactions with her surroundings.
- Name each section in the story.
- Draw connections to the subject's reactions as a result of these experiences.

Harm and Healing

Strategy: Readers of biographies notice who the subject surrounds him- or herself with.

As You Read . . .
- Think about the people and groups that the subject chooses to connect with.
- Ask: *Why would the subject seek out these people?*
- Think about how the people and groups she has chosen to connect with impact her life.

Places to Pause
Pause after the pages in which Jennifer finds community with other individuals who also have disabilities. Share your reflections about Jennifer and the community's sense of identity and how they came together to protest for equal rights. Make connections to how, within this group's activism, Jennifer finds inclusion and purpose with those who are similar to and different from her.

Circle Questions
Say to students: *We notice that Jennifer finds a community of people who are similar to her and welcome her. What are some of the ways Jennifer built relationships with others? Share your thinking aloud.*

Afterwards, invite students to reflect by saying: *Think about your classmates' reflections. Share one or two new things you learned from what others shared.*

SKILLS AND STANDARDS

Comprehension Skill:
Consider the subject/character's perspective

CCSS: RI.3.2, RI.3.3, RI.3.7, RI.3.8 • SL.3.1, SL.3.4 • RI.4.2, RI.4.3, RI.4.7, RI.4.8 • SL.4.1, SL.4.4

Social Justice:
DI.3-5.6 (I like knowing people who are like me and different from me, and I treat each person with respect.)

CASEL:
Relationship Skills
- Develop positive relationships

Responsible Decision-Making
- Evaluate personal, interpersonal, community, and institutional impacts

Carryover Coaching

Use these additional prompts for one-on-one conferences.

- Think about the subject's identity and how she is similar to others.
- Make a list of connections the subject has made with others in her community.

SKILLS AND STANDARDS

Comprehension Skill:
Identify cause and effect

CCSS: RI.3.2, RI.3.3, RI.3.7, RI.3.8 • SL.3.1, SL.3.4 • RI.4.2, RI.4.3, RI.4.7, RI.4.8 • SL.4.1, SL.4.4

Social Justice:
JU.3-5.15 (I know about the actions of people and groups who have worked throughout history to bring more justice and fairness to the world.)

CASEL:
Responsible Decision-Making
- Identify solutions for personal and social problems
- Reflect on one's role to promote personal, family, and community well-being

Relationship Skills
- Stand up for the rights of others

♥ Heartwork

Strategy: Readers think about how personal experiences and the needs of others motivate the subject of our biographies.

As You Read . . .
- Think about the subject's personal experiences.
- Think about what she wants for others.
- Make connections between the subject's experiences and desires and her actions.
- Look for ways the subject's actions impact her and her community.

Places to Pause

Pause on the page that shows Jennifer climbing the steps of the U.S. Capitol Building. Thinking aloud, share your reflections about how many people were telling her to stop yet she continued to take action and move up the steps. Share your thinking about how Jennifer feels motivated when she thinks about her own experiences and of those who are like her. Provide students with an example of her reflecting on being shut out of the cafeteria at school.

Circle Questions

Say to students: *We see Jennifer take action for justice when she climbs the stairs of the U.S. Capitol Building. How did Jennifer's history-making actions inspire and lead to change?*

Afterwards, invite students to reflect by saying: *After reflecting on what everyone has shared about Jennifer's story, think about other changes we'd all like to make, both big and small.*

Carryover Coaching

Use these additional prompts for one-on-one conferences.

- List what you know about the subject's identity and her actions.
- Make connections to the subject's actions and her motivations.
- Draw upon these connections to deepen your understanding.

 Beyond the Book

As we read through this powerful story of action, community, and change for justice, we notice that the main subject, Jennifer, was a child during these historic moments of courage. As a class, conduct research on a few child activists who are fighting for change in the present day. You may read some stories or articles together. Emphasize that these activists are children who are leading for change in these very moments. Then, have students work in groups to research a child activist and create a presentation about them and their accomplishments to present to the rest of the class.

SKILLS AND STANDARDS

CASEL:
Self-Management
- Exhibit self-discipline and self-motivation
- Set personal and collective goals
- Show the courage to take initiative
- Demonstrate personal and collective agency

Students brainstorm other people who have fought for positive change.

A Few More Favorites

When Charley Met Emma by Amy Webb

We Move Together by Kelly Fritsch and Anne McGuire

BIRDSONG

Written and illustrated by Julie Flett
Grades 3–4 / Fiction / #OwnVoices

A Bit About the Book

This heartwarming Cree story captures the beauty of friendship and empathy across the ages. As we turn the pages, we read about a young girl who befriends her elderly neighbor. They connect through their love of nature and art, and their friendship blossoms throughout the seasons. Over time, the reality of aging takes its course, and the young girl's wisdom, empathy, and action bring peace and love to her close friend. This book creatively includes Cree words and their meanings throughout the story.

SKILLS AND STANDARDS

Comprehension Skill: Infer about character relationships

CCSS: RL.3.1, RL.3.2, RL.3.3, RL.3.4, RL.3.5 • SL.3.1, SL.3.4 • RL.4.1, RL.4.2, RL.4.3, RL.4.4, RL.4.5 • SL.4.1, SL.4.4

Social Justice:
DI.3-5.9 (I feel connected to other people and know how to talk, work, and play with others even when we are different or when we disagree.)

CASEL:

Self-Awareness
- Integrate personal and social identities
- Link feelings, values, and thoughts

Social Awareness
- Recognize strength in others

 ## Identity

Strategy: Readers know that our identities are a combination of many things, including our interests, experiences, and culture. Our identities help us connect with others through shared similarities and interests.

As You Read . . .
- Observe the similarities and differences between the characters.
- Ask: *What are some pieces of the characters' identities?*
- Reflect and share about the characters' identities and the pieces they have in common.

Places to Pause

Pause on the page in which Agnes shows Katherena the pottery she has been working on that resembles the moon phases. Think aloud about the similarities between the two characters: their love for nature and for creating art. Then share your thinking about their differences, specifically focusing on their ages. Model your thinking as you make the connection that even though their ages are vastly different, they can still build a relationship based on shared interests and similarities.

Circle Questions

Say to students: *Let's think back to all the ways Agnes and Katherena connect with each other based on their similarities and shared interests. Write about the activities the characters do together. Then share aloud about the connections you made between these actions and the bond between them.*

Afterwards, invite students to reflect by saying: *After reading this book, we noticed that even though there's a big difference in their ages, the characters connect based on a common interest they hold as part of their identity. Think about a moment when you connected with someone because they shared a part of your identity, even though you may also have some differences. Then share about your connection and the parts of your identities that are the same and different.*

Carryover Coaching
Use these additional prompts for one-on-one conferences.
- Look closely at the pages.
- Look at the characters' shared actions.
- Draw a connection between the shared actions and the characters' relationship with each other.

 Harm and Healing

Strategy: Readers know that we can learn lessons from watching the ways characters build connections over time.

As You Read . . .
- Observe the characters' interactions with each other across the pages.
- Notice how the characters' interactions change throughout the story.
- Ask: *What can that teach me about connections with others over time?*

Places to Pause
Read over the pages in which Katherena meets Agnes for the first time. Share what you notice about Katherena in the picture at the beginning (e.g., her hands are behind her back, or her arms are by her side). Then read the page again about their shared interest over art and nature. Model your thinking as you observe Katherena smiling as she waves goodbye after Agnes tells her to visit again soon. Think aloud about how you notice the characters building a connection over time, even though they started out as strangers.

Circle Questions
Say to students: *Let's think about the relationship between Katherena and Agnes from the beginning of the book to the end. What do you think the characters learned throughout this story?*

Afterwards, invite students to reflect by saying: *What did someone share that you also thought about already? What did someone share that you hadn't thought of yet?*

Carryover Coaching
Use these additional prompts for one-on-one conferences.
- Find a part in the book in which the characters' relationship grows.
- Think: *What is happening here?*
- Look for what changed.
- Name how the expressions on each character's face change over time.

SKILLS AND STANDARDS

Comprehension Skill:
Analyze character change

CCSS: RL.3.1, RL.3.2, RL.3.3, RL.3.4, RL.3.5 • SL.3.1, SL.3.4 • RL.4.1, RL.4.2, RL.4.3, RL.4.4, RL.4.5 • SL.4.1, SL.4.4

Social Justice:
DI.3-5.6 (I like knowing people who are like me and different from me, and I treat each person with respect.)

CASEL:
Social Awareness
- Develop positive relationships
- Practice teamwork and collaborative problem-solving

SKILLS AND STANDARDS

Comprehension Skill:
Infer about character

CCSS: RL.3.1, RL.3.2, RL.3.3, RL.3.4, RL.3.5 • SL.3.1, SL.3.4 • RL.4.1, RL.4.2, RL.4.3, RL.4.4, RL.4.5 • SL.4.1, SL.4.4

Social Justice:
AC.3-5.16 (I pay attention to how people [including myself] are treated, and I try to treat others how I like to be treated.)

CASEL:
Social Awareness
- Understand and express gratitude
- Demonstrate empathy and compassion
- Show concern for the feelings of others
- Recognize situational demands and opportunities

Heartwork

Strategy: Readers develop a deeper understanding of the characters by connecting to moments when they showed empathy and action.

As You Read . . .
- Name an action by the character.
- Remember a time when you've shown empathy and acted similarly.
- Ask: *How did this make you feel?*
- Make a connection to understand what we can learn about the character.

Places to Pause
Pause on the page in which Katherena understands that Agnes is growing weaker and shares an idea. Model your thinking as you draw a connection between Katherena's understanding of Agnes's health and the actions she decides to take to help her friend.

Circle Questions
Say to students: *At the end of the book, we saw Katherena demonstrate compassion and empathy for Agnes through her actions, such as sharing her artwork and sitting by Agnes's side. What can we learn about Katherena from these moments? Write down your reflections.*

Afterwards, invite students to reflect by saying: *Think of a moment from your life that can help you connect deeper with Katherena. What was your moment of compassion and empathy in supporting someone else?* To keep the circle time brief, offer students a sentence stem, such as: "When I . . ."

Carryover Coaching
Use these additional prompts for one-on-one conferences.
- Think about the character's actions.
- Think back to a time when you took action to show someone else empathy and compassion.
- Feel that feeling again.
- Pretend you're the character.
- Feel the character's feelings as you think about what is happening.

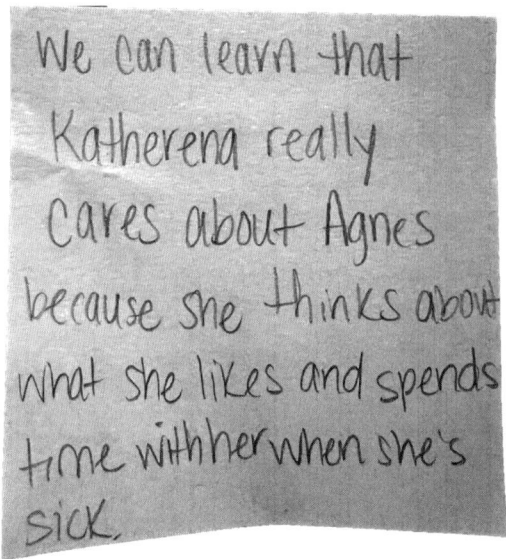

A student's reflection on the connection between Katherena and Agnes.

70 • Read-Alouds With Heart: Grades 3–5

 Beyond the Book

Through this beautiful story of friendship and empathy, we learned the power of making connections through our similarities, regardless of any differences. This is a wonderful moment to invite your classroom community to find connections across the ages. With permission from your school, reach out to a local nursing home or senior center. Begin to build relationships between your students and the seniors to demonstrate the power of connection through similarities. Through video calls, writing letters, or even visits, if possible, invite students to share about themselves with the elders and find ways to build relationships. This emphasizes the importance of empathy, understanding, and mutual respect.

SKILLS AND STANDARDS

CASEL:
Social Awareness
- Demonstrate empathy and compassion
- Show concern for the feelings of others
- Recognize situational demands and opportunities

A Few More Favorites

Drawn Together
by Minh Lê

A Different Pond
by Bao Phi

DIGGING FOR WORDS:
José Alberto Gutiérrez and the Library He Built
Written by Angela Burke Kunkel / Illustrated by Paola Escobar
Grades 3–4 / Biography / #OwnVoices

A Bit About the Book
The exquisite illustrations of Paola Escobar transport us straight into the barrio of La Nueva Gloria, Colombia, where we meet two Josés. The first is a young boy passing the time until his favorite day, Saturday. The second is José Alberto Gutierrez, a garbage collector from Bogota, Colombia. This José's passion for books and community, along with his practice of collecting unwanted books from the wealthier neighborhoods, led him to building his own library and offering his community the wonderful gift of the written word. On Saturdays, young José, along with dozens of others, rush to the Paradise library. There they pore over stacks of books that José curated and go on adventures all over the world—through pages. This book highlights the power we all have to make a difference in our communities. Turn to the final pages for more information on José Alberto Gutiérrez and his contributions to ensure that people have access to books.

SKILLS AND STANDARDS
Comprehension Skill:
Analyze subject/character

CCSS: RL.3.1, RL.3.3 • RI.3.1 • SL.3.1.A–C, SL.3.2, SL.3.6 • RL.4.1, RL.4.3 • RI.4.1 • SL.4.1.A, B, D; SL.4.2; SL.4.6

Social Justice:
JU.3-5.15 (I know about the actions of people and groups who have worked throughout history to bring more justice and fairness to the world.)

CASEL:
Relationship Skills
• Stand up for the rights of others

 Identity
Strategy: Readers of biographies pay close attention to how a person's job helps shape his identity.

As You Read . . .
- Pause in parts that describe what the subject does for a living.
- Ask: *How does his job connect to what he wants and what he does?*
- Consider how the subject's job adds to his identity and whether it played a role in what makes him famous.

Places to Pause
Pause on the page that shows José driving the garbage truck with a stack of books next to him. Model your thinking by talking about how José uses his job to collect books for himself and others and how that helped him build a library for his community. Be sure to connect not only his job but also the choices he made and the ways he used his profession to create something wonderful.

Circle Questions
This circle offers students an opportunity to transfer the strategy in a broader sense. Say to them: *Think about another famous person whom you've read about. How did they use their job to help them make a change?*

Afterwards, invite students to reflect by saying: *Let's add the people we heard about to our to-read lists. Which people and jobs sounded interesting to you? Who might you want to read about next?*

Carryover Coaching
Use these additional prompts for one-on-one conferences.
- Find sections that show the subject at work.
- Think about whether his work ties to his goals.
- Consider how his job offers him opportunities for changing or helping.

Harm and Healing

Strategy: Readers of biographies look for ways the subject contributed to his community.

As You Read . . .
- Track the actions of the subject.
- Think about how he contributed to a cause or to a group of people.
- Put together the actions of the subject and his impact on a cause or community.

Places to Pause
Pause on the last page with the author's note. Thinking aloud, list José's actions on the board or chart paper: finding a book for himself, looking for books on his route, creating a library, starting a foundation, speaking at conferences. Share an idea that comes to mind about how José's actions helped so many people gain access to books. Offer students one of these sentence stems: "[Subject] helped [group] by [action]." Or, "[Subject] changed people's lives by [action]." For example: "José helped the people in his community by giving them access to books."

Circle Questions
Say to students: *Think about what creating the library did for José and the people in his community. How might José's library have changed their lives?*

Afterwards, invite students to reflect by asking: *What did someone share that helped you see José's library in a brand-new way?*

Carryover Coaching
Use these additional prompts for one-on-one conferences.
- List some of the subject's actions.
- Create a timeline, noting important actions.
- Look across the actions for a pattern that ties to the bigger change the subject made.
- Think about who was impacted by the subject's choices and how their lives were changed.

SKILLS AND STANDARDS

Comprehension Skill:
Identify problem and solution

CCSS: RL.3.3, RL.3.5 • RI.3.3 • SL.3.1.A–C, SL.3.2, SL.3.6 • RL.4.3, RL.4.5 • RI.4.3 • SL.4.1.A–C, SL.4.2, SL.4.6

Social Justice:
JU.3-5.15 (I know about the actions of people and groups who have worked throughout history to bring more justice and fairness to the world.)

CASEL:
Social Awareness
- Recognize situational demands and opportunities

Responsible Decision-Making
- Reflect on one's role to promote personal, family, and community well-being
- Evaluate personal, interpersonal, community, and institutional impacts

SKILLS AND STANDARDS

Comprehension Skill: Consider subject/character's perspective

CCSS: RL.3.3, RL.3.6 • RI.3.3 • SL.3.1.A–C, SL.3.2, SL.3.6 • RL.4.3, RL.4.6 • RI.4.3, RI.4.5 • SL.4.1.A–C, SL.4.2, SL.4.6

Social Justice:
DI.3-5.10 (I know that the way people are treated today, and the way they have been treated in the past, is part of what makes them who they are.)

CASEL:

Self-Awareness
- Identify one's emotions
- Demonstrate honesty and integrity
- Link feelings, values, and thoughts

Social Awareness
- Take others' perspectives
- Recognize strengths in others

 Heartwork

Strategy: Readers of biographies study the perspectives of their subject to understand what motivated the subject to contribute.

As You Read . . .
- List things you know about the subject's life.
- Look for things that seem to be important to the subject.
- Find connections between the subject's life, what is important to him, and his actions and contributions.

Places to Pause
Pause on the page that shows José in the imaginary jungle created from his reading. Think aloud about what we knew about José's life—he left school early, he became a bricklayer and garbage collector, he read with his mom every night, he found a book that he read over and over. Then, share your thoughts about José's perspective about books—he loves books because they provide an escape or a way to travel to other times and places. His love of books must have pushed him to want others to have those experiences, too.

Circle Questions
José Gutierrez named his foundation *La Fuerza de las Palabras* or The Strength of Words. Ask students: *What does that say about his beliefs about books?*

Afterwards, invite students to reflect by asking: *What ideas did your classmates share that stand out to you most?*

Carryover Coaching
Use these additional prompts for one-on-one conferences.
- List what you know about the subject.
- Use what you know about the subject to think about what was important to him.
- Consider: *Was he trying to help someone/something? Did he see something as unfair? Did he want to become an expert at something?*
- Put his actions and his interests together. What does that make you think?

📖 Beyond the Book

In *Digging for Words,* we see how one man's series of small actions changed the lives of many in his community. His decisions to contribute stemmed from something that gave him joy and his willingness to take advantage of opportunities that presented themselves. In this activity, invite students to think about their interests, talents, and opportunities to plan for ways they might contribute to their communities. Revisit the story to introduce the idea of contribution. Then, offer students a strategy for how we might be mindful of ways we can contribute. Be sure to stress that contributions don't have to be huge undertakings. A contribution can be something as small as offering someone a compliment, or something big, like organizing a food drive.

Say to students: *People can make contributions by looking for opportunities that allow them to share their strengths and/or act in ways that will help others.*

- *Think about something that brings us joy and/or something that we are good at.*
- *Imagine how we might use our talent to offer something to our community, whether it be help, entertainment, or resources.*
- *Make a plan that connects opportunities to contribute—what you can offer and what that will look like.*

After introducing and modeling the strategy, divide the class into groups and have students talk about and imagine different ways they can contribute to their class, school, family, or neighborhood community. Afterwards, invite students to share their plans in a circle. Alternatively, create something in your classroom, such as a contributions board, that keeps the conversation about contributions present.

A Few More Favorites

Preaching to the Chickens: The Story of Young John Lewis by Jabari Asim

The Crayon Man: The True Story of the Invention of Crayola Crayons by Natascha Biebow

SKILLS AND STANDARDS

CASEL:
Responsible Decision-Making
- Reflect on one's role to promote personal, family, and community well-being

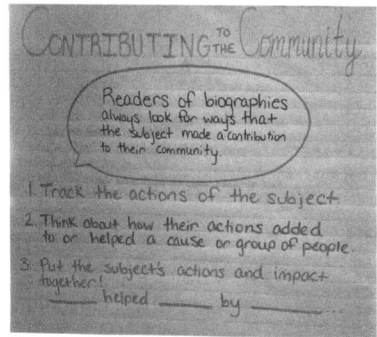

Things to consider as students read the book.

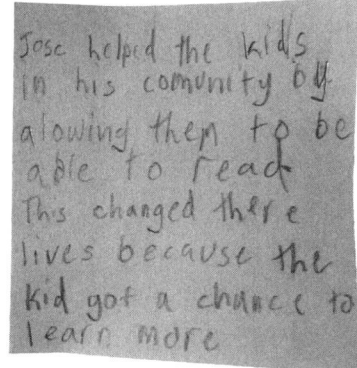

A student's reflection on how Jose's actions changed lives.

DREAMERS
Written and illustrated by Yuyi Morales
Grades 4–5 / Narrative / #OwnVoices

A Bit About the Book
Inspired by the author's personal journey, this colorful book tells the story of a mother and her young child who dream of creating a new life in a new country. This book celebrates hope and resilience as they migrate to and navigate an unfamiliar world. We follow the character and her child as they face challenges, stay determined, and follow their dreams. Lyrical text and beautiful illustrations guide readers through the courage of leaving a familiar home to finding the light in a new one.

SKILLS AND STANDARDS

Comprehension Skill:
Analyze character

CCSS: RL.4.1, RL.4.3, RL.4.4 • SL.4.1, SL.4.4 • RL.5.2, RL.5.3, RL.5.4 • SL.5.1, SL.5.4

Social Justice:
ID.3-5.3 (I know that all my group identities are part of who I am, but none of them fully describes me and this is true for other people too.)

CASEL:

Self-Awareness
- Integrate personal and social identities
- Have a growth mindset
- Develop interests and a sense of purpose

Responsible Decision-Making
- Reflect on one's role to promote personal, family, and community well-being

 **Identity**

Strategy: Readers understand that our identities are often shaped by our relationships.

As You Read . . .
- Pause in parts that show the character with people she cares about.
- Think about how the character's feelings for each person play a role in what she does and what she wants.
- Name how the character's relationships play a role in her identity.

Places to Pause
Pause on the page in which the character and her child pack their bags and start their journey toward a new life in a new country. Think aloud about the bond between the mother and child. Model your reflection by sharing how you noticed that the part of the character's identity as a mother motivates her to begin on a journey for a better life for her and her child.

Circle Questions
Say to students: *Let's look at the first page where we see the character say to her child, "I dreamed of you." This connects deeply with the character's identity that is shaped by her family. Write down your reflections on the character's feelings about setting out on this journey with her child for a new life.*

Afterwards, invite students to reflect by saying: *Think about those whom you are close to—whether family, caregivers, friends, or role models. In what ways do your actions support the wellness of yourself and those whom you are close to? Write down your actions and motivations.*

Carryover Coaching
Use these additional prompts for one-on-one conferences.
- Reflect on the character's relationship with her family or loved ones.
- Think about how the character's identity has an impact on the actions she takes for those whom she cares about.
- Consider how our identities have an impact on the things we do for our loved ones.

Harm and Healing

Strategy: Readers analyze the challenges and hardships a character experiences based on her group's identity and where she is from.

As You Read . . .
- Make note of the character's expressions during challenging moments.
- List the situations where the character came face to face with hardships.
- Ask: *What were some moments during which the character experienced hardship because of her identity?*

Places to Pause
Pause on the page where you see the character and her child looking at a map and playing in the fountain. Share your reflections about the hardships and challenges the character experiences. Think aloud about the connection between her identity and her actions. Model how you analyze the character's expressions and what she might be feeling in these moments.

Circle Questions
Say to students: *Look closely at the main character's expression and share what we can tell about her feelings and experiences in these moments of challenges. Now, let's look closely at her child's face in these moments, too. What do we observe about the child's feelings? Let's look together at the page with the writing in the sky. Write down your reflections, including the characters' expressions and the scene.*

Afterwards, invite students to reflect by saying: *Take a moment to think about how the expressions on someone's face help you understand how that person feels. Share your reflections aloud.*

Carryover Coaching
Use these additional prompts for one-on-one conferences.
- Look at the actions and experiences over time and across the pages.
- Take note of the character's experiences and notice any patterns.
- Think about how they impacted the character's life and the steps she took.

SKILLS AND STANDARDS

Comprehension Skill:
Identify problem and solution

CCSS: RL.4.1, RL.4.3, RL.4.4 • SL.4.1, SL.4.4 • RL.5.2, RL.5.3, RL.5.4 • SL.4.1, SL.4.4 • SL.5.1, SL.5.4

Social Justice:
JU.3-5.14 (I know that life is easier for some people and harder for others based on who they are and where they were born.)

CASEL:
Social Awareness
- Identify diverse social norms, including unjust ones
- Understand the influences of organizations and systems on behavior

SKILLS AND STANDARDS

Comprehension Skill:
Consider character's perspective

CCSS: RL.4.1, RL.4.3, RL.4.4 • SL.4.1, SL.4.4 • RL.5.2, RL.5.3, RL.5.4 • SL.5.1, SL.5.4

Social Justice:
DI.3-5.9 (I feel connected to other people and know how to talk, work, and play with others even when we are different or when we disagree.)

CASEL:
Self-Management
- Set personal and collective goals
- Show the courage to take initiative

 **Heartwork**

Strategy: Readers notice how characters help each other through hard times.

As You Read . . .
- Think about the challenges the character has faced.
- Look at the people surrounding the character. Think about how they may have offered support or comfort.
- Name ways the secondary characters or the community eased the challenges felt by the main character.

Places to Pause

Pause on the page where the character shares, "Where we didn't need to speak, we only needed to trust." Think aloud about the character's hardships throughout the story and what this sentence means in connection with the character entering the library. Share your thinking about the library being a place of comfort and community. Model your thinking about the significance of the illustrations and the people the character meets. Think aloud about the character's feelings and experiences as she discovers connection, community, and a feeling of home.

Circle Questions

Read again the pages in which the character starts to say, "Someday we will become something we haven't even yet imagined . . ." to the end of the book. Invite students to take a moment to connect to the author's words: "We are dreamers . . ." Ask them: *What dreams did this mother have for herself and her child?* Have them reflect on her journey.

Afterwards, invite students to reflect by saying: *Let's take a moment to hold space for the character overcoming hardships. Take a deep breath in, hold the breath, and slowly exhale out. Place a hand on your heart to imagine the feeling of connection and community. Take another soft breath in and out.*

Carryover Coaching

Use these additional prompts for one-on-one conferences.
- Look across the pages.
- Notice how the character's expressions and illustrations change across the pages.
- Make a connection to the character's experiences and her expressions.

📖 Beyond the Book

While reading this beautiful story, we learned about hope and courage and creating a feeling of belonging through the character's journey of resilience. With the class, reread the last two pages together: "We are stories. We are two languages. We are *lucha* (fighters). We are resilience. We are hope. We are dreamers of the world." Together as a class, brainstorm words that represent who you are as dreamers. Record these on a chart. Then invite students to decorate the chart by adding colors and images that represent your class community. Display the chart in the classroom, on your door, or in the hallway.

> **SKILLS AND STANDARDS**
>
> **CASEL:**
> Self-Management
> - Set personal and collective goals
> - Show the courage to take initiative

A Few More Favorites

Carmela Full of Wishes
by Matt de la Peña

La Frontera
by Alfredo Alva and Deborah Mills

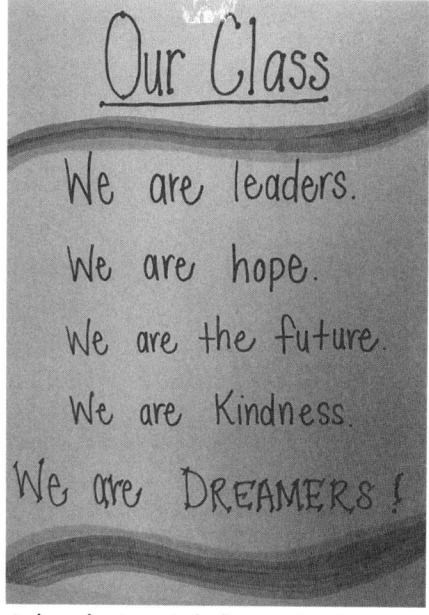

A class chart created after reading *Dreamers*

FAUJA SINGH KEEPS GOING
Written by Simran Jeet Singh / Illustrated by Baljinder Kaur
Grades 4–5 / Biography / #OwnVoices

A Bit About the Book
This beautiful biography of Fauja Singh, the first 100-year-old marathoner, tells the story of an amazing man who never takes no for an answer. Fauja's challenges begin during his first years of life as he struggles to walk and suffers through the hurtful words from the local kids' teasing and taunting. But from early on, Fauja's belief in himself and his motivation to succeed help him overcome every obstacle in his path. We follow him through life as he becomes a happy farmer and father. Following the death of his beloved wife, he uproots his life in Punjab to begin again in London with his children. As an octogenarian, he discovers his passion for running. Fauja Singh becomes a record-holding marathoner! His story is an inspiration to all who read it. Note: Don't skip the foreword by Fauja Singh himself. He shares more of his story and offers words of encouragement directly to the readers.

SKILLS AND STANDARDS

Comprehension Skill:
Analyze subject/character

CCSS: RL.4.1, RL.4.3 • RI.4.1, RI.4.3 • SL.4.1.A, B, D; SL.4.2; SL.4.6 • RL.5.1, RL.5.3 • RI.5.1, RI.5.3 • SL.5.1.A, B, D; SL.5.2; SL.5.6

Social Justice:
JU.3-5.13 (I know that words, behaviors, rules, and laws that treat people unfairly based on their group identities cause real harm.)

JU.3-5.15 (I know about the actions of people and groups who have worked throughout history to bring more justice and fairness to the world.)

CASEL:
Self-Awareness
 • Examine prejudices and biases

Social Awareness
 • Identify diverse social norms, including unjust ones

Identity

Strategy: Biography readers notice when a subject's actions challenge people's assumptions and expectations.

As You Read . . .
 • Look for a part in which other people make assumptions about what a person can do based on his identities.
 • Pay close attention to what the subject does next.
 • Ask: *Have the subject's actions proved those people wrong? How has this subject helped people move away from their biases?*

Places to Pause
Pause on the page that shows Fauja talking to reporters about running in the NYC marathon. Think aloud about how people didn't believe in him because of his age. You might even point out the notes on the clipboard saying he's weak. Then, look ahead to Fauja's next actions. Talk about how he then ran and finished the marathon, even if it wasn't his personal best. Share your thoughts about how his finishing proved the reporters wrong, but more important, how it pushed back on ageism (when people assume someone can't do something because of his or her age).

Circle Questions
Invite students to think back across Fauja Singh's life. You may decide to reread the whole text or do a picture walk across the pages. Say to students: *Think*

about all the times that Fauja was teased and told he couldn't do something. What message did he send by doing it anyway? After everyone has shared, create a timeline of Fauja's life that pinpoints moments when he challenged assumptions and biases.

Afterwards, invite students to reflect by saying: *Think about all the ways Fauja challenged bias and take a moment to appreciate what he's accomplished.*

Carryover Coaching
Use these additional prompts for one-on-one conferences.
- Look for moments when the subject is not allowed to do something or told he can't.
- Zoom in on what the subject says next and think about whether his response pushes back against bias.
- Look across the pages that follow and connect what he does. Think about how his actions connect to pushing back on what was said.

Harm and Healing

Strategy: Readers study the subject/character's mindset when facing challenges.

As You Read . . .
- Find a moment of challenge for the subject.
- Pay close attention to what the subject says, thinks, and does in those moments.
- Ask: *Based on the way he responds, what mindset does he bring to this challenge? How does this help or make it worse?*

Places to Pause
Pause on the page that shows Fauja walking for the first time as a child. As you think aloud, point out the parts that show him listening to his mother's words of encouragement, ignoring others' words, and practicing again and again. Share how this helps you see that Fauja has a "can-do" mindset. This mindset helps push him forward, and his determination pays off!

Circle Questions
Say to students: *Think about the feelings that Fauja experiences during this moment of conflict and harm. How are bias and injustice causing harm here?*

Afterwards, invite students to reflect by saying: *Think of another story that this book may have reminded you of. Write about a connection you made to another situation you have experienced, witnessed, or heard about through that other story.*

SKILLS AND STANDARDS

Comprehension Skills: Consider subject/character's perspective

CCSS: RL.4.1, RL.4.3 • RI.4.2 • SL.4.1.A, B, D; SL.4.2 • RL.5.1, RL.5.3 • RI.5.1 • SL.5.1.A, B, D; SL.5.2

Social Justice:
AC.3-5.17 (I know it's important for me to stand up for myself and for others, and I know how to get help if I need ideas on how to do this.)

CASEL:
Self-Awareness
- Link feelings, values, and thoughts

Self-Management
- Exhibit self-discipline and self-motivation
- Set personal and collective goals

Carryover Coaching

Use these additional prompts for one-on-one conferences.

- Look for parts in which other people are teasing or telling the subject he can't do something.
- Study the subject's response: his facial expressions, his thoughts, his words, his actions.
- Think: *What does his response say about how he thinks about problems? What does his response say about what he believes? What does his self-talk say about his mindset?*
- Connect the subject's mindset to his success or failure.

SKILLS AND STANDARDS

Comprehension Skills:
Analyze subject/character; determine a call to action

CCSS: RL.4.1, RL.4.3 • RI.4.1, RI.4.3 • SL.4.1.A, B, D; SL.4.2; SL.4.6 • RL.5.1, RL.5.3 • RI.5.1, RI.5.3 • SL.5.1.A, B, D; SL.5.2; SL.5.6

Social Justice:
AC.K-2.17 (I can and will do something when I see unfairness—this includes telling an adult.)
AC.K-2.18 (I will say something or tell an adult if someone is being hurtful, and will do my part to be kind even if I don't like something they say or do.)
AC.K-2.19 (I will speak up or do something if people are being unfair.)

CASEL:
Responsible Decision-Making
- Reflect on one's role to promote personal, family, and community well-being
- Evaluate personal, interpersonal, community, and institutional impacts

---

♥ Heartwork

Strategy: Readers are inspired by the subjects in their biography books.

As You Read . . .

- Name some of the admirable traits that helped the subject succeed.
- Choose a trait that you might want for yourself.
- Imagine yourself with that same trait.
- Ask: *What might I do differently?*

Places to Pause

Pause on the page at the end of the book that shows Fauja holding up his medal. Reflect aloud about some of his admirable traits, and then choose one that you might want for yourself. Share what having that trait would look like in your life. Set a goal to be more like that each day.

For example, you might say: *Fauja has so many wonderful traits. He's forgiving, determined, brave, and strong. I really admire his determination. It helped him when things were hard and people told him he couldn't do something. I want to be more determined, just like him. Let me picture myself being determined. I've been training to ride my bike, but sometimes I give up on hills and walk my bike up the hill instead. When I'm on my bike next time, I'm going to think of Fauja and say to myself, "You can do it. Stay on the bike!" I'm going to keep going just like he would.*

Circle Questions

Ask students: *What do you admire most about Fauja?* You can end here with admiration. If you want to extend this to action, however, you can ask an additional question: *What might Fauja inspire you to do or try?*

Afterwards, invite students to reflect by saying: *Reflect on what your classmates shared. Think about how one person's actions can inspire us in so many ways. Think about what sticks most with you and how you may choose to do something differently now that you've read the story and listened to your classmates' ideas.*

Carryover Coaching

Use these additional prompts for one-on-one conferences.
- List the subject's accomplishments.
- Think about the traits that helped him do something wonderful.
- Ask: *Which trait do I value most?*
- Picture yourself with that trait and watch a "mind movie" of yourself doing something with that trait.
- Notice what you look and sound like as you act with this trait.
- Set an intention: *What will I do differently?*

Beyond the Book

Throughout the book, we hear the words of Fauja's mother replay in his mind. He calls upon her wisdom from his early years, teaches her motivating words to his own children as they grow, and brings back her words as a source of motivation even in his old age. Sometimes bits of advice from people we love can have a huge impact across our whole life. Invite students to think about words of encouragement they've heard and use them as mini mantras that they can call upon again and again when they face hard times. Through shared writing, create a mantra poster or advice mantras on sentence strips that you can hang around the room. Model using the mantras when you're in need, and remind students to use them, too.

Say to students: *Fauja's mother told him, "You know yourself and what you're capable of. Today is a chance to do your best." Those wonderful words became advice that he lived by. Each time he met a challenge, Fauja reminded himself of his mother's words. Let's all think of advice that we've heard. What good advice helped you through tough times? Let's turn our best advice into mantras to help us each day, too.*

A Few More Favorites

Emmanuel's Dream: The True Story of Emmanuel Ofosu Yeboah by Laurie Ann Thompson

The Girl and the Bicycle by Mark Pett

SKILLS AND STANDARDS

CASEL:
Self-Management
- Manage one's emotions
- Identify and use stress-management strategies

Classroom T-chart showing people's assumptions about Fauja across his life and how he used actions to push back against those assumptions.

THE FEARLESS FLIGHTS OF HAZEL YING LEE

Written by Julie Leung / Illustrated by Julie Kwon
Grades 3–4 / Biography / #OwnVoices

A Bit About the Book

This riveting book tells us the true story of Hazel Ying Lee, a brave woman who was determined to follow her dreams of becoming a pilot. As a Chinese American woman, she fought through barriers and pursued her goals, despite what others said to try to stop her. She dedicated her life and fought on the frontlines of World War II as part of the Women Airforce Service Pilots (WASPs). Hazel overcame many hardships she faced, and her legacy continues to represent justice and inspiration. Read this beautiful biography of an empowering woman who helped change the world.

SKILLS AND STANDARDS

Comprehension Skill:
Analyze subject/character

CCSS: RI.3.2, RI.3.3, RI.3.7, RI.3.8 • SL.3.1, SL.3.4 • RI.4.2, RI.4.3, RI.4.7, RI.4.8 • SL.4.1, SL.4.4

Social Justice:
JU.3-5.14 (I know that life is easier for some people and harder for others based on who they are and where they were born.)

CASEL:

Self-Awareness
- Integrate personal and social identities
- Link feelings, values, and thoughts
- Examine prejudices and biases
- Have a growth mindset
- Develop interests and a sense of purpose

Self-Management
- Exhibit self-discipline and self-motivation
- Show the courage to take initiative

Identity

Strategy: Readers can learn about a subject by studying how she reacts when she is treated in unfair ways.

As You Read . . .
- Pause in the parts in which people treat the subject poorly or with bias because of her identity.
- Ask: *How does the subject's identity impact the actions she can take or experiences she can have?*
- Name how the subject reacts in the face of bias and injustice based on her identity.

Places to Pause

Pause on the page in which Hazel and her fellow WASPs test out newly manufactured planes and resolve defects. Review the pages that lead up to this part of the story. Think aloud about Hazel's dream, her motivation, and the messages she received along the way.

Circle Questions

Say to students: *Think about the messages Hazel received throughout her journey as she followed her dreams. Many of these messages had to do with her identity. We read that she was treated unfairly because she was Chinese American and female. How did these messages impact Hazel?*

Afterwards, invite students to reflect by saying: *Let's think about how even today we might still hear messages like those, in which some people are treated unfairly or not given the same opportunities because of their identity. Write down some of those stereotypes and biases.*

Carryover Coaching

Use these additional prompts for one-on-one conferences.
- Find sections that show the subject's expressions after facing biases and injustice.
- Think about the subject's actions as a result of these experiences.

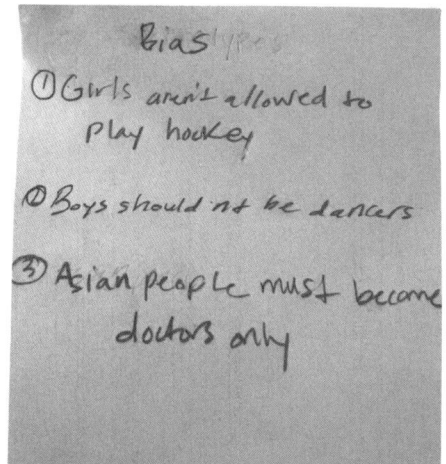

Students brainstorm some biases we still hear today.

Harm and Healing

Strategy: Readers of biographies think about how the subject's group identities make being or doing certain things harder.

As You Read . . .
- Pause in parts in which the subject faces harm from others' actions.
- Think about the subject's experience with her identity and the group identities that are causing this harm.

Places to Pause

Pause on the page in which Hazel's plane has crash-landed on a field in Kansas and she has to defend herself against an angry farmer. Think aloud about Hazel's feelings and actions during these moments. Reflect on the illustrations on the page that show the farmer holding a pitchfork and Hazel ducking under her plane.

Circle Questions

Say to students: *Think about the feelings that Hazel experienced during this moment of conflict and harm. How are bias and injustice causing harm here?*

Afterwards, invite students to reflect by saying: *Think of another story that this book may have reminded you of. Write about a connection you made to another situation you have experienced, witnessed, or heard about through that other story.*

Carryover Coaching

Use these additional prompts for one-on-one conferences.
- List the subject's experiences.
- Look closely at the pictures to make connections to the subject's feelings.
- Think about how the subject was impacted by the actions of others.

SKILLS AND STANDARDS

Comprehension Skill: Consider subject/character's perspective

CCSS: RI.3.2, RI.3.3, RI.3.7, RI.3.8 • SL.3.1, SL.3.4 • RI.4.2, RI.4.3, RI.4.7, RI.4.8 • SL.4.1, SL.4.4

Social Justice:
JU.3-5.13 (I know that words, behaviors, rules, and laws that treat people unfairly based on their group identities cause real harm.)

CASEL:

Social Awareness
- Identify diverse social norms, including unjust ones

Responsible Decision-Making
- Identify solutions for personal and social problems
- Evaluate personal, interpersonal, community, and institutional impacts

SKILLS AND STANDARDS

Comprehension Skill:
Identify problem and solution

CCSS: RI.3.2, RI.3.3, RI.3.7, RI.3.8 • SL.3.1, SL.3.4 • RI.4.2, RI.4.3, RI.4.7, RI.4.8 • SL.4.1, SL.4.4

Social Justice:
JU.3-5.15 (I know about the actions of people and groups who have worked throughout history to bring more justice and fairness to the world.)

CASEL:
Responsible Decision-Making
- Identify solutions for personal and social problems
- Reflect on one's role to promote personal, family, and community well-being

Relationship Skills
- Resolve conflicts constructively
- Stand up for the rights of others

Heartwork

Strategy: Readers look at the direct impacts of a subject's contributions at the time of the action and today.

As You Read . . .
- List the subject's contributions and achievements.
- Think about how the subject's contributions made life better at the time.
- Ask: *How have her contributions laid a path for continued change that we can still see today?*

Places to Pause
Pause on the page that shows Hazel's family coming together to write a letter to President Franklin Roosevelt. Share your thinking about how Hazel's perseverance impacted those around her, her fellow WASPs, and the country's Air Force at the time. Then share your reflection on how her contributions had an impact on the world today, and how she set the path for Asian women and all women to follow their dreams.

Circle Questions
Say to students: *We see the author writes that Hazel's family "willed the world to move forward for Hazel, and won." What does the word* forward *mean here? Sit with the feelings that Hazel's family felt. Write about how you think Hazel would have felt about her family's actions.*

Afterwards, invite children to reflect by saying: *Reflect on what your classmates shared. What ideas that were shared stand out to you most?*

Carryover Coaching
Use these additional prompts for one-on-one conferences.
- List what you know about the experiences the subject faced.
- Make connections to the subject's actions and those of the other subjects.
- Draw upon these connections to deepen your understanding.

 Beyond the Book

In this beautiful story, we learn about the brave and fearless Hazel Ying Lee. In describing Hazel, the story quotes a Cantonese saying: "She was born fearless, she was not afraid of wind or water." We learn about Hazel's determination, strength, and the hardships she faced through many injustices rooted in bias and prejudice. Even through this, she persevered until the end of her life. Hazel's family fought to ensure her contributions and life were celebrated. As a class, engage in a mindful practice to connect our heartwork to Hazel's story.

Invite students to sit comfortably with a hand on their heart or on their lap. Connect to the story of Hazel, remembering her contributions and the challenges she fought against. Take a deep breath in together and exhale out together. Repeat this breath practice two more times. Then invite students to remember Hazel's story in standing up for justice and continuing to persevere, even in the face of challenges.

A Few More Favorites

It Began With a Page: How Gyo Fujikawa Drew the Way
by Kyo Maclear

Drum Dream Girl: How One Girl's Courage Changed Music
by Margarita Engle and Rafael López

SKILLS AND STANDARDS

CASEL:

Self-Management
- Manage one's emotions
- Identify and use stress management strategies

IN OUR MOTHERS' HOUSE
Written and illustrated by Patricia Polacco
Grade 5 / Fiction

A Bit About the Book

Like many things in life, *In Our Mothers' House* is both beautiful and imperfect. Patricia Polacco weaves a gorgeous tale about building a family and the love felt by all within the walls of their home. The family's story unfolds as the narrator, one of the grown siblings, shares snippets from her childhood memories. From the joy that came with each new baby being adopted to the care taken in sewing custom-made Halloween costumes and rolling out homemade gnocchi with Nonno, the love in the household shines through every page. And the memories, both joyous and hurtful, give readers a window into their family's traditions, celebrations, and hardships.

While there is much to love about this book, we also invite students to critique some of the author's choices. The two moms in this story share a similar style and are described as being uncomfortable wearing dresses, which can reinforce stereotypes. Instead of avoiding the text, we're choosing to use it to teach students to recognize stereotyping in the books that they read and to think about other choices that could have been made by the author.

SKILLS AND STANDARDS

Comprehension Skill:
Critique author's craft

CCSS: RL.5.6, RL.5.7 • SL.5.1.A–D, SL.5.6

Social Justice:
JU.3-5.11 (I try and get to know people as individuals because I know it is unfair to think all people in a shared identity group are the same.)

CASEL:
Self-Awareness
• Examine prejudices and biases

Relationship Skills
• Demonstrate cultural competency

 Identity

Strategy: Readers critique books by thinking about whether the author crafted characters that reinforce stereotypes.

As You Read . . .
- Take a close look at the way the author describes the characters. Look closely at the pictures as well.
- Ask: *Does this description make it seem like all people who share an identity look or act a certain way?*
- Acknowledge when stereotyping is present. Then, consider other ways the author could have written about the characters.

Places to Pause

Pause on the page that shows Meema and Marmee making the dresses for the tea. Think aloud about how the author chose to make both characters dislike wearing dresses. Then, look closely at the images of the characters, taking notice of their short hair. Share how those ideas and images may send an untrue message that all homosexual women look and dress a certain way. Imagine for a moment another way that the characters could have looked or been described that would not have reinforced that stereotype.

Circle Questions

After acknowledging the stereotypical images of the moms in the story, invite students to reimagine a different mom character who might replace one of the mothers in the story. Say to students: *Let's reimagine one of the mom characters in the book to erase the stereotypical image. Draw or write a short description. Then, let's share our new possibilities with one another.* Give students a few minutes to work.

Afterwards, invite students to reflect by saying: *Think about all the different ways we reimagined the character. Now, think about yourself as a writer. What lessons might you take back with you as you create characters?*

Carryover Coaching

Use these additional prompts for one-on-one conferences.
- Make a mental picture of the character using the author's words.
- Think about whether the image you see would upset someone who shares that identity.
- Think about whether the image you see is not true for everyone, but the book makes it seem that way.

A fifth grader reimagines Marmee to push back on the character stereotyping.

Harm and Healing

Strategy: Readers consider the repercussions of a character's unkind acts.

As You Read . . .
- Notice when a character does something unkind.
- Think about how that act hurt both the person causing harm and those being harmed.
- Name the impacts on everyone involved.

Places to Pause

Pause on the page that shows Mrs. Lockner confronting Meema and Marmee on the day of the block party. Think aloud about how hurtful Mrs. Lockner's comments were and how they caused harm to so many. Talk about the confrontation causing fear, confusion, and pain for the family as well as isolation for Mrs. Lockner and her family. Share how everyone involved is hurt by the hateful action of Mrs. Lockner.

Circle Questions

For this circle, zoom in on the Lockner children. Invite students to think about the different ways that Mrs. Lockner's actions toward Meema and Marmee have hurt her own children. Say to students: *Unkindness can hurt in many*

SKILLS AND STANDARDS

Comprehension Skill:
Analyze character

CCSS: RL.5.1, RL.5.3 • SL.5.1.A–D, SL.5.6

Social Justice:
JU.3-5.13 (I know that words, behaviors, rules, and laws that treat people unfairly based on their group identities cause real harm.)

CASEL:
Self-Awareness
- Examine prejudices and biases

Social Awareness
- Demonstrate empathy and compassion
- Show concern for the feelings of others

different ways. Think about Mrs. Lockner's actions. How did her actions toward Meema and Marmee negatively impact her children?

Afterwards, invite students to reflect by asking: *What was shared that helped you see other ways the kids were affected? How does that impact your understanding of the depth of the harm caused by Mrs. Lockner?*

Carryover Coaching
Use these additional prompts for one-on-one conferences.
- Look beyond who the character was talking to.
- Notice other characters who may also be impacted by her words.
- Think about how the character's actions impact relationships, limit opportunities, or set a poor example for others.

SKILLS AND STANDARDS

Comprehension Skill:
Read with empathy

CCSS: RL.5.3, RL.5.7 • SL.5.1.A–D, SL.5.6

Social Justice:
AC.3-5.16 (I pay attention to how people [including myself] are treated, and I try to treat others how I like to be treated.)

CASEL:
Self-Awareness
- Identify one's emotions

Social Awareness
- Demonstrate empathy and compassion
- Show concern for the feelings of others

Heartwork

Strategy: Readers know that people's facial expressions and body movements reveal a lot about their emotions.

As You Read . . .
- Look for descriptions of facial expressions and body movements within the text. (Use pictures, too, if available.)
- Create a mind movie of the way the character's body looks and moves.
- Think about the emotions your mental image raises. What emotions do the character's body movements convey to you?

Places to Pause
Pause on the pages that show the kids getting the puppies. While this is an obvious example, it also provides a space for a clear demonstration that uses both words and images. Highlight the sentences describing the moment the puppies were put into the children's hands and spend a minute or two looking closely at the physical movement and expressions shown in the pictures. Think aloud about the joy and excitement that comes through clearly as the reader studies the words and images together.

Circle Questions
Use this circle opportunity for students to do a bit of their own descriptive "show, not tell" writing. Zoom in on the pages that show the family adopting Will and Millie. Give students a few minutes to think about the situation, look closely at the illustrations, and then write a sentence or two describing the characters' facial and/or body movements. Say to students: *Let's step into the author's shoes and do a bit of writing that would show the characters' emotions. Pick one character. Pay close attention to what she's doing and her face in the picture. Make the picture move in your mind. Then, write a sentence*

or two that would "show, not tell" her emotion. We'll come back to share our sentences in the circle in a few minutes.

Afterwards, invite students to reflect by saying: *Reflect on the descriptions your classmates shared and think about some of the language that really helped you connect to the character's emotions. Think about ways you might bring these ideas and even language into your own writing.*

Carryover Coaching

Use these additional prompts for one-on-one conferences.
- Read a description and make your own body match the description.
- Think about how you feel when your body looks that way.
- Reread the description and picture the body in motion.
- Put the description and the situation together to think about what the character must be feeling.

Beyond the Book

This activity teaches students how to engage in restorative circles. This is not meant to be a one-time experience. Rather, it is intended to teach a practice that can help students resolve conflict and heal hurt feelings. Restorative circles should be practiced again and again so that they might be more effective when students need to use them to resolve real-life issues.

To support effective communication, we will tap into the power of restorative circle questions. Begin by talking to students about how the family experienced hurt because of identity-based prejudice. Explain that we try to learn more about one another to prevent this kind of harm, and we are trying to help people understand how much their actions can hurt others. Understanding how we've hurt others often leads to people being more aware of others' feelings and prevents us from repeating hurtful actions. When someone does something unkind, one way to help them understand how their actions hurt others is by using circle questions that highlight the way their choices impact someone else and what that person needs to do to make things right.

Say to students: *Let's brainstorm some ways we might see unkindness at school. Then, we'll pretend we are in those situations and use our questions to help us understand one another and heal the hurt.* Try one of these starter scenarios:
- During lunch, a child goes to sit in an empty seat at a table. When the child attempts to sit, someone at the table says the seat is taken and then moves their bag to the spot. All the other kids at the table laugh.
- At lunch, someone makes a comment about the food another child brings. They may make a face when the child opens his lunch bag or say something like, "Ugh! You eat that?!"

SKILLS AND STANDARDS

CASEL:
Relationship Skills
- Communicate effectively
- Practice teamwork and collaborative problem-solving
- Resolve conflicts constructively

- Someone shares a secret with a friend because they trust them and wants advice. Instead, the friend tells the secret to everyone in the class.

Invite students to role-play both the child who was harmed and the child who caused the harm. Ask these questions to the child who was harmed: *What did you think when you realized what was happening? What impact does this incident have on you and others? What has been the hardest thing for you? What do you think needs to happen to make things right?*

Ask these questions to the child who caused the harm: *What happened? What were you thinking of at the time? What have you thought about since? Who has been affected by what you have done? In what way have they been affected? What do you think you need to do to make things right?*

These role-play experiences can help students be more thoughtful in the moment. They are also great practice so that students understand how to use these questions as a guide to fixing problems that do arise. For more information on restorative circles, visit https://www.iirp.edu/news/time-to-think-using-restorative-questions.

A Few More Favorites

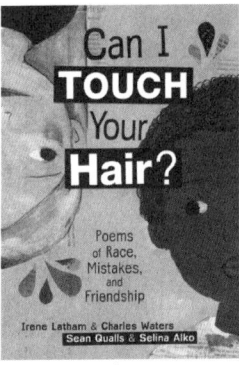

Can I Touch Your Hair?
by Charles Waters and Irene Latham

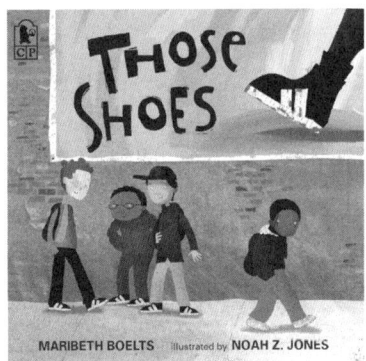

Those Shoes
by Maribeth Boelts

THE JOURNEY
Written and illustrated by Francesca Sanna
Grades 4–5 / Fiction

A Bit About the Book
The harsh realities of war have ripped away this family's beautiful life by the sea. After the loss of their father and the chaos and uncertainty brought about by their new life, Mom plans the family's escape. Told through the heart and perspective of a child, this story takes readers on a journey through the darkness and across land and sea as Mom and her children flee the only home they've ever known to find safety and a new beginning.

 ## Identity

Strategy: Readers consider how different parts of a person's identity play a role in their decisions and actions.

As You Read . . .
- Think about the identities of the characters.
- Consider how their identities may tie to their choices.
- Ask: *Do the characters' identities carry benefits or create challenges for them? How?*

Places to Pause
Pause on the page that shows the family packing. Model your thinking about how the mother's role as parent and protector influenced her decision to move the family.

Circle Questions
Zoom in on either the mother or a child character in this story. Take a moment to map out some of their identities. Ask students: *How might different aspects of the mother's or children's identities have influenced their actions and decisions?* Alternatively, you might ask: *How might life be harder for them because of a specific part of their identity?*

Afterwards, invite students to reflect by asking: *What ideas that were shared stand out to you most?*

Carryover Coaching
Use these additional prompts for one-on-one conferences.
- Think about what a character just did or chose to do.
- Look at the interaction between the character and another person.
- List the identities of the character.
- Connect the character's identity to their choice.
- Explain how their identity influenced what they did.

SKILLS AND STANDARDS

Comprehension Skill:
Analyze character

CCSS: RL.4.1, RL.4.3 • SL.4.1.A–D, SL.4.6 • RL.5.1, RL.5.3 • SL.5.1.A–D, SL.5.6

Social Justice:
JU.3-5.14 (I know that life is easier for some people and harder for others based on who they are and where they were born.)

CASEL:
Social Awareness
- Recognize situational demands and opportunities
- Understand the influences of organizations/systems on behavior

SKILLS AND STANDARDS

Comprehension Skill:
Analyze character

CCSS: RL.4.1, RL.4.3 • SL.4.1.A–D, SL.4.6 • RL.5.1, RL.5.3 • SL.5.1.A–D, SL.5.6

Social Justice:
JU.3-5.13 (I know that words, behaviors, rules, and laws that treat people unfairly based on their group identities cause real harm.)

CASEL:
Social Awareness
- Demonstrate empathy and compassion
- Show concern for the feelings of others
- Recognize situational demands and opportunities

Harm and Healing

Strategy: Readers know that we can understand characters deeply by studying how they deal with both internal and external struggles.

As You Read . . .
- Think about the experiences of the characters in the book.
- Ask: *What were some of the physical challenges they faced? What were some of the emotional challenges they faced?*
- Explore how the characters dealt with those struggles. Think about what it says about them as people.

Places to Pause
Pause on the page that shows the angry guard yelling at the family to go back. Model your thinking about the physical and emotional strain of the journey on them at this point. Talk about the physical exertion as well as the emotional weariness tied to the fear of getting caught.

Circle Questions
Say to students: *Think about the children's experiences. What were some of the physical challenges they faced on their journey? What were some of the emotional challenges they faced as they left their friends, belongings, and lives behind? What have we learned about them based on the way they dealt with those struggles?*

Afterwards, invite students to reflect by asking: *What did someone share that helped you see something in a brand-new way?*

Carryover Coaching
Use these additional prompts for one-on-one conferences.
- Think about what's happening in the story. What is in the character's way?
- Push into the character's heart. Think about how the struggle impacts her emotionally.
- Notice what the character does in response to her challenges.
- Write or say what you are learning about the character.

 **Heartwork**

Strategy: Readers analyze the images in a text and consider the mood that those images evoke, or bring out in them.

As You Read . . .
- Look closely at the image on a page to study the emotion of the picture.
- Think about the colors and styles used to create the picture. Connect that to the content.
- Ask: *How do the illustrations help tell the emotional journey of these characters? How do the images in this book influence your feelings and response?*

Places to Pause
Pause on the pages that show the shadow hands ripping away their former life. Think aloud about how the shadow tearing away at their family time at the beach or their time in their home adds a feeling of devastating loss.

Circle Questions
Say to students: *Think about the artwork in this book. Let's zoom in on the use of color and size. How did the images help you connect to the feelings of the mother and her children? How did these images influence your feelings and response?*

Afterwards, invite children to reflect by asking them how they may bring the ideas they heard into creating art or writing. Ask: *What new thing can you try when you're creating? What do you now wonder about or want to learn more about?*

Carryover Coaching
Use these additional prompts for one-on-one conferences.
- Look at the use of color. What feelings do the color choices project?
- Study the subject. Name what you see in the image.
- Tie the story to the image. How do the emotions of the story and image connect?

SKILLS AND STANDARDS

Comprehension Skill: Analyze images for tone and mood

CCSS: RL.4.3, RL.4.7 • SL.4.1.A–D, SL.4.6 • RL.5.3, RL.5.7 • SL.5.1.A–D, SL.5.6

Social Justice:
JU.3-5.13 (I know that words, behaviors, rules, and laws that treat people unfairly based on their group identities cause real harm.)

CASEL:
Self-Awareness
- Identify one's emotions

Social Awareness
- Demonstrate empathy and compassion
- Show concern for the feelings of others

SKILLS AND STANDARDS

CASEL:

Social Awareness
- Recognize situational demands and opportunities
- Demonstrate empathy and compassion
- Show concern for the feelings of others

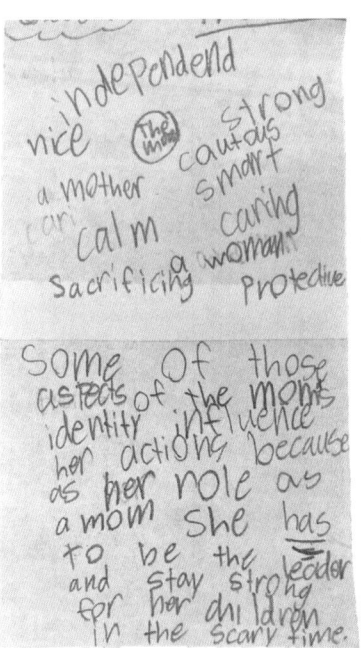

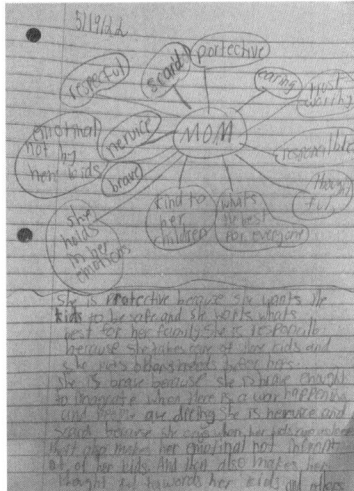

A student maps out the mother's identities and reflects on how they influenced her decisions and actions.

Beyond the Book

This book gives us a little glimpse into some of the experiences of refugee children. While every person's experience is different, we know that everyone who finds themselves in a new place wants to feel comfortable and to feel like they belong. Invite students to consider ways their community could welcome a refugee child to their school/class.

Say to students: *Let's think about ways we might welcome a student whose experience is like the children in this book into our community. We'd want our new friend to feel welcome, but not pressured. How might we get ready to welcome this friend into our community?*

Here are some additional supports for teachers welcoming refugee students into their communities:

- https://www.learningforjustice.org/magazine/spring-2017/immigrant-and-refugee-children-a-guide-for-educators-and-school-support-staff
- https://www.unhcr.org/en-us/teaching-about-refugees.html

A Few More Favorites

My Name is Jorge: On Both Sides of the River
by Jane Medina

One Green Apple
by Eve Bunting

MANGO MOON
Written by Diane de Anda / Illustrated by Sue Cornelison
Grades 4–5 / Realistic Fiction / #OwnVoices

A Bit About the Book
In *Mango Moon,* we experience the emotional and physical devastation 10-year-old Maricela feels as she is separated from her father. After Papi is taken to a detention center to await deportation, Maricela steps into her new reality. This reality rips away the familiar, causing her mother to take on a second job and forcing them to move in with family and Maricela to start at a new school. Throughout the book, we see Maricela trying to look at the bright side whenever possible. She looks forward to sharing a room with her cousin and spends time making notes and gifts for Papi. But she can't help but feel overwhelmed by his loss. This poignant story captures a too-familiar tale of fear and heartbreak. **Note:** This book is available in both Spanish and English.

 Identity

Strategy: Readers consider how different parts of a character's identity can be a source of joy or a reason for him or her to be harmed or targeted.

As You Read . . .
- Zoom in on one character.
- Ask: *Were there moments when a part of this character's identity was celebrated? Were there moments when this person was treated unfairly or hurt because of who he or she is?*
- Think about what this helps you understand about that person's life.

Places to Pause
Pause on the page that shows Mama and the children on the couch with the green card. Walk students through your thinking about how Papi was sent away because of his identity as an undocumented immigrant. (Depending on students' prior knowledge, you may need to share more about what this means.) Think aloud about how his being taken from his family and sent to another country because of his immigration status caused him and his family heartache.

Circle Questions
Say to students: *As this family deals with the realities of Papi's deportation, they experience many different emotions and changes in their lives. After reading, what do you realize about the impact that Papi's removal has on this family?* Offer this sentence stem to students: "Papi's deportation caused . . ."

SKILLS AND STANDARDS

Comprehension Skill:
Analyze character

CCSS: RL.4.1, RL.4.3 • SL4.1.A–C, SL.4.2, SL.4.6 • RL.5.1, RL.5.3 • SL.5.1.A-C, SL.5.2, SL.5.6

Social Justice:
JU.3-5.13 (I know that words, behaviors, rules, and laws that treat people unfairly based on their group identities cause real harm.)

CASEL:
Social Awareness
- Take others' perspectives
- Demonstrate empathy and compassion
- Identify diverse social norms, including unjust ones

Afterwards, invite students to reflect by asking: *What did someone share that made you think, "Me too!"? What did someone share that helped you see something in a brand-new way?*

Carryover Coaching

Use these additional prompts for one-on-one conferences.
- Think about how the character's identity connects to how he or she is being treated.
- Consider whether the treatment is fair or right.
- Ask: *What does this make me realize?*

Harm and Healing

Strategy: Readers look for a problem snowball—what at first seems like one problem grows into many problems.

As You Read . . .
- Look for the moment when things begin to go wrong.
- Follow the events that come after that moment.
- Use a timeline to track how the problem grows, who it affects, and how it affects them.

Places to Pause

Pause on the page that shows the little girl and her brother looking out the window at a bird in a tree. Think aloud about how we found the main problem in the first few pages: Papi was taken away. Soon, however, we see that this problem leads to more problems: Mama has to work more, and the kids can't play outside after school. Create a timeline on chart paper and place a dot on the timeline for each problem. Write the problem above the dot on the timeline. Underneath the dot, jot down who it affects and how it affects them.

Circle Questions

Say to students: *There were so many things that happened to this family after Papi was taken to the detention center. Right now, think of one snowball problem—a new problem that happened because of the original problem—and how it hurt the characters.* Offer this sentence stem to students: "Another problem that came up was ____. It hurt the characters because ____."

Afterwards, invite students to reflect by asking: *What thoughts that were shared stood out most to you? What new idea do you have because of what someone else shared?*

SKILLS AND STANDARDS

Comprehension Skill:
Identify problem and solution

CCSS: RL.4.1, RL.4.3 • SL.4.A–C, SL.4.2 • RL.5.1, RL.5.2, RL.5.3 • SL.5.1.A–C, SL.5.2

Social Justice:
JU.3-5.14 (I know that life is easier for some people and harder for others based on who they are and where they were born.)

CASEL:
Social Awareness
- Demonstrate empathy and compassion
- Show concern for the feelings of others

Carryover Coaching
Use these additional prompts for one-on-one conferences.
- Look for the main problem earlier in the story.
- Ask: *What happened right after the problem?*
- Look for secondary problems caused by the initial issue.
- Consider new stresses, new responsibilities, or changes that happened because of the problem.

 **Heartwork**

Strategy: Readers look for objects that may connect to a deeper meaning or symbolize a feeling or idea.

As You Read . . .
- Look for objects that the author describes in detail or repeats throughout the book.
- Notice what the character is doing, saying, thinking, and feeling when that object shows up in the story.
- Ask: *What meaning does this object hold? Does this object symbolize a feeling or idea?*

Places to Pause
One recurring image in this text is the "mango moon." Share with students that you noticed the moon many times across the pages. Go back to revisit the pages in which the moon appears. Think aloud about how on pages that show the moon, we see the little girl with or thinking about Papi. The moon seems to be a reminder of Papi—its brightness showing their love. Seeing it up in the sky reminds the girl that they are still connected even when they are far apart.

Circle Questions
Before asking students to share in the circle, revisit the book by doing a picture walk across the pages. Tell students as you revisit the pictures to keep an eye out for an object that seems to repeat or hold a deeper meaning. Say: *Let's revisit the pictures across the pages of this book. Be on the lookout for an object that you feel has a deeper meaning or represents an important idea in the story. Once you choose something, get ready to tell us the object and what you think it means in the story.* Offer this sentence stem to students: "One object that stood out was ____. I think it represents ____."

Afterwards, invite students to reflect by asking: *What did someone share that helped you see something in a brand-new way?*

SKILLS AND STANDARDS

Comprehension Skill:
Identify symbolism

CCSS: RL.4.1, RL.4.3 • SL.4.1.A–C, SL.4.2 • RL.5.1, RL.5.2, RL.5.3 • SL.5.1.A–C, SL.5.2

Social Justice:
ID.3-5.2 (I know about my family history and culture and about current and past contributions of people in my main identity groups.)

CASEL:
Social Awareness
- Take others' perspectives
- Demonstrate empathy and compassion
- Show concern for the feelings of others

Carryover Coaching
Use these additional prompts for one-on-one conferences.
- Notice any objects that keep showing up in the story.
- Notice a spot where the author shares details about an object.
- Think: *What is the object connected to? What feelings fit with the object or how the character connects to the object?*
- Name the object as a symbol. Say: "[Object] represents ____."

SKILLS AND STANDARDS

CASEL:
Self-Awareness
- Identify one's emotions

Beyond the Book

Invite students to expand their emotional vocabulary. Having the language to articulate our own emotions and name the emotions of others is key to our ability to self-regulate and empathize. In her book *Atlas of the Heart*, Brené Brown writes, "Language is our portal to meaning-making, connection, healing, learning, and self-awareness. Having access to the right words can open up entire universes" (2022). The work of this section requires multiple sessions. Because most people (children and adults) narrow their description of emotion to three words—*happy, sad,* and *mad*—we might start with the associated emotions tied to those. In the upper grades, we might graduate to tapping into some of the words in *Atlas of the Heart*. Learning the language of emotions is ongoing work that should begin in primary grades and continue across a child's educational experience. Below, find a brief description of one way you might introduce the meaning of each feeling word and help students associate those words with facial expressions and stories.

- Say the feeling word to students and invite them to repeat the word with you; for example: *insecurity*.
- Then, share a child-friendly definition of the word. *(Feeling insecure can mean feeling unsure whether your needs will be met or whether you'll be accepted. You might be doubting yourself and thinking, "Am I enough?" You may also be doubting that others will be able to give you what you need and asking yourself, "Will I be okay?")*
- Next, tell a story about a time when you felt the emotion. *(Let me think about a time I felt insecure . . .)*
- Invite students to remember a story of the feeling, too. *(Think of a time when you may have felt insecure or seen someone feeling insecure in a movie/TV show/book.)* Share what the feeling might look like on our bodies. *(Let's picture what insecure looks like on our bodies. What does your face look like? What does your body look like?)*
- Listen to and reinforce ideas, such as hanging your head down, making your body smaller, slumping your shoulders, and so on. Have children practice sharing their own definitions of the word. *(Think about our stories around the word* insecure. *If someone asked you what the word* insecurity *means, what would you say?)*

As an option, create a growing chart through interactive writing with the word, student-created definitions, and an image of a person feeling that way. Invite students to illustrate their feeling word stories.

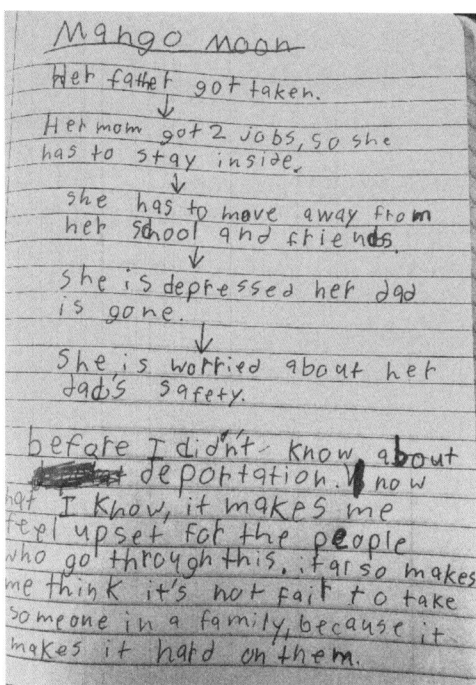

A student lists how a problem in the story snowballed into more problems.

A Few More Favorites

The Day Saida Arrived
by Susana Gómez Redondo

Four Feet, Two Sandals
by Karen Lynn Williams and Khadra Mohammed

PRIDE:
The Story of Harvey Milk and the Rainbow Flag
Written by Rob Sanders / Illustrated by Steven Salerno
Grades 4–5 / Biography

A Bit About the Book
This brilliant and colorful book shares the empowering story of social activist and political leader Harvey Milk. He dreamed of a better world and a better tomorrow, and he set out with ambition and hope to turn those dreams into a reality. With the support of a few people, Milk worked through challenges and overcame many obstacles in the fight for equal rights for the LGBTQ+ community. As we turn the pages, we hear about the historical unfurling and life of the Pride flag and its representation of hope for millions of LGBTQ+ people across the globe. This story of hope, activism, and pride is sure to lift our spirits and remind us of the power of our voices.

SKILLS AND STANDARDS

Comprehension Skill:
Analyze character

CCSS: RI.4.2, RI.4.3, RI.4.7, RI.4.8 • SL.4.1, SL.4.4 • RI.5.2, RI.5.3, RI.5.7, RI.5.8 • SL.5.1, SL.5.4

Social Justice:
JU.3-5.13 (I know that words, behaviors, rules, and laws that treat people unfairly based on their group identities cause real harm.)

CASEL:
Self-Awareness
- Integrate personal and social identities
- Examine prejudices and biases
- Have a growth mindset
- Develop interests and a sense of purpose

Responsible Decision-Making
- Identify solutions for personal and social problems
- Reflect on one's role to promote personal, family, and community well-being

---

 ## Identity

Strategy: Readers pay attention to how a subject's words can lead to change.

As You Read . . .
- Pause in places that show the subject speaking, especially to large groups.
- Listen to his words for clues to the changes he wants.
- Ask: *How does what the subject says help move toward change?*

Places to Pause
Pause on the pages that show Harvey Milk revealing the Pride flag at the march and then Milk marching in front of the crowd. Share your thinking about Milk's leadership with the community and the fight for equality. Using Milk's motivational words, model your thinking about finding ways to engage in activism within our communities, our laws, and in our personal lives.

Circle Questions
Say to students: *We see Harvey Milk as an activist and politician trying to bring about change. Let's reread the quote: "Rights are won only by those who make their voices heard." What does Milk's message mean here? How do his actions express his message? What does this mean for the LGBTQ+ community?*

Afterwards, invite students to reflect by saying: *Think about the power of our voices. What does it mean to speak up? Write about a time when you used your voice to make an impact (or how you hope to use your voice in the future). Reflect on what others have shared.*

Carryover Coaching

Use these additional prompts for one-on-one conferences.
- Look for a part that shows the subject talking about his beliefs/desires.
- Think about how the subject's identities impact the actions he can take.
- Consider how his identities led him to recognize his responsibility to take action.

Harm and Healing

Strategy: Readers use a timeline to understand what motivates a subject or character to make change.

As You Read . . .
- Take note of the timeline of the events, including accomplishments and challenges.
- Ask: *What were some of the reasons that motivated the subject to challenge injustice?*
- Ask: *What do you understand about why the subject moved toward change?*

Places to Pause
As you read the pages, create a timeline of important events. Model your thinking aloud about Milk's actions through the pages. Share the connections between the injustices Milk observed and the effect those had on the actions he took toward fighting against injustice.

Circle Questions
Say to students: *We see the word* hope *created with Pride flags after the assassination of Harvey Milk. Reflect on this question: How did the community respond after Milk's death? Write and share your responses.*

Afterwards, invite students to reflect by saying: *Even after Harvey Milk's death, other people carried on his dream for equality and flying the colorful flag continued. Let's pause and sit with the feelings that the community had in their hearts to keep fighting. Hold this feeling. Share your reflections.*

Carryover Coaching
Use these additional prompts for one-on-one conferences.
- Look at the events that happened over time.
- Take note of all the characters and their responses to the events.
- Think about the actions they took as a result of events of hardship or accomplishment.

SKILLS AND STANDARDS

Comprehension Skill: Consider subject/character's perspective

CCSS: RI.4.2, RI.4.3, RI.4.7, RI.4.8 • SL.4.1, SL.4.4 • RI.5.2, RI.5.3, RI.5.7, RI.5.8 • SL.5.1, SL.5.4

Social Justice:
AC.3-5.17 (I know it's important for me to stand up for myself and others, and I know how to get help if I need ideas on how to do this.)

CASEL:
Self-Management
- Set personal and collective goals
- Show the courage to take initiative

Social Awareness
- Identify diverse social norms, including unjust ones
- Understand the influences of organizations and systems on behavior

SKILLS AND STANDARDS

Comprehension Skill:
Identify problem and solution

CCSS: RI.4.2, RI.4.3, RI.4.7, RI.4.8 • SL.4.1, SL.4.4 • RI.5.2, RI.5.3, RI.5.7, RI.5.8 • SL.5.1, SL.5.4

Social Justice:
AC.3-5.19 (I will speak up or do something when I see unfairness, and I will not let others convince me to go along with injustice.)

CASEL:
Relationship Skills
- Practice teamwork and collaborative problem-solving
- Resolve conflicts constructively
- Stand up for the rights of others

 **Heartwork**

Strategy: Readers analyze the importance, meaning, and representation of symbols for characters' identity groups.

As You Read . . .
- Think about the challenges the characters have faced from biases and prejudices.
- Reflect on the ways the characters overcome these challenges through their belief in a symbol.
- Consider how a symbol provides a feeling of importance and purpose for the characters.

Places to Pause
Pause at the page that shows the mile-long Pride flag being carried during a march for equality. Model your reflection about the powerful message of this symbol for LGBTQ+ individuals. Share and model your thinking about how the flag represents a message of hope, equality, and a demand for change.

Circle Questions
Reread the page that shows the mile-long Pride flag being carried. We see the words of Harvey Milk: "I ask for the movement to continue, for the movement to grow." Say to students: *Think about what this message means and why he shared these empowering words. Share aloud.*

Afterwards, invite students to reflect by asking: *What ideas that were shared stand out to you most?*

Carryover Coaching
Use these additional prompts for one-on-one conferences.
- Look across the pages.
- Reflect on the importance and meaning of symbols.
- Make connections to the characters' responses to the symbols.

104 • Read-Alouds With Heart: Grades 3–5

📖 Beyond the Book

After reading the story of Harvey Milk and the Pride flag, circle back to the discussion of activism, leadership, and anchoring change/hope to a symbol. With your students, research a variety of symbols that have represented similar meaning. Invite students to brainstorm a social issue they are passionate about. Working on their own or collaboratively, have students conduct research and design and create a symbol, poster, or banner that stands for change/hope/pride for their issue of choice. Students can choose to present and speak about their symbol to the class, the school, and the community. Empower students by displaying this work within the classroom and hallways and leading an activism march through the school as students carry their symbols with pride.

SKILLS AND STANDARDS

CASEL:
Relationship Skills
- Communicate effectively
- Demonstrate cultural competency
- Practice teamwork and collaborative problem-solving
- Stand up for the rights of others

A student-created poster based on *Pride: The Story of Harvey Milk and the Rainbow Flag*.

A Few More Favorites

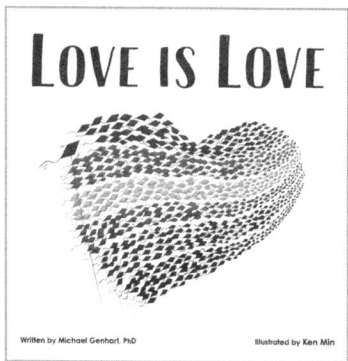

Love Is Love
by Michael Genhart, PhD

Malala's Magic Pencil
by Malala Yousafzai

THE PROUDEST BLUE:
A Story of Hijab and Family
Written by Ibtihaj Muhammad, with S. K. Ali / Art by Hatem Aly
Grades 3–4 / Realistic Fiction / #OwnVoices

A Bit About the Book
This story starts with the joy of first experiences as we meet Faizah and her sister, Asiya, who is getting ready to start her school year in her very first hijab. The girls shop for the perfect color hijab, settling on a gorgeous blue—the color of the sea and sky. As they step out on the first day of school and walk over together, Faizah sees her sister as a beautiful princess. Yet when they arrive, not all the students respond to her sister's hijab with the same admiration. Faizah watches as students react with a mixture of curiosity, acceptance, and rejection. This story, written by the first female Muslim American Olympic medal winner, gives readers a window into the author's experience and teaches important lessons about bullying, self-love, and taking pride in who we are.

SKILLS AND STANDARDS

Comprehension Skill:
Analyze character

CCSS: RL.3.1, RL.3.3 • SL.3.1.A–C, SL.3.2, SL.3.6 • RL.4.1, RL.4.3 • SL.4.1.A, B, D; SL.4.2; SL.4.6

Social Justice:
ID.3-5.1 (know and like who I am and can talk about my family and myself and describe our various group identities.)
DI.3-5.8 (I want to know more about other people's lives and experiences, and I know how to ask questions respectfully and listen carefully and non-judgmentally.)

CASEL
Self-Awareness
- Integrate personal and social identities
- Identify personal, cultural, and linguistic assets
- Identify one's emotions

(continued)

 Identity

Strategy: Readers compare themselves to characters by looking for similarities and differences in their identities and experiences.

As You Read . . .
- Focus on one character whom you'd like to compare yourself to.
- Ask: *What do we share?*
- Pay attention to what the character looks like, her problems, her experiences, and her feelings. Think about how your lives are different.
- Think about how your similarities and differences help you understand the character.

Places to Pause
Pause on the page that shows Faizah drawing a picture of her and her sister as princesses. Every teacher's think-aloud for this strategy will sound different because it will depend on their personal identities as compared with Faizah's identities. As you think aloud about how you compare with Faizah, be sure to talk about both a similarity and a difference. Then, explore how these connections and differences help you understand the character. For example, Dana might say that like Faizah, she loves drawing and imagining herself and her family in different ways. One difference is that because Dana is part of an interracial family, when she draws her family, they all look different. Her husband and sons have tan skin and dark curly hair, and she has peachy skin and salt-and-pepper straight hair.

Circle Questions

Say to students: *Take a moment to think about Faizah, the little sister in the story. What's something you both have in common? How does that help you understand her or her feelings?*

Afterwards, invite students to reflect by saying: *In listening to all the connections between us and our character, what connections do you realize you also share with one another?*

Carryover Coaching

Use these additional prompts for one-on-one conferences.
- Zoom in on one character.
- Take a moment to study the picture and how the character is described.
- Make a mental image of the character. Notice whether the person may share physical characteristics with you.
- Think about the character's feelings and experiences in the story and think about your feelings in similar moments.
- Consider how those shared experiences help you understand the character's perspective.

> **CASEL** (continued)
> **Social Awareness**
> - Take others' perspectives
> - Recognize strengths in others
> - Show concern for the feelings of others

Harm and Healing

Strategy: Readers identify the problem among characters in a story and push themselves to think about what caused the problem in the first place.

As You Read . . .
- Look for a part that shows a problem among characters.
- Ask: *What feelings, misunderstandings, or needs are causing this problem?*
- Explore some possible causes to create a theory about why this might be happening.

Tip: When building these types of theories, start your idea with *maybe*. This sets up readers to continue looking for evidence to prove or disprove their idea and gives them a bit of grace in acknowledging that we don't know for sure.

Places to Pause

Pause on the pages that show the shadowy characters pointing and laughing at Asiya in her new hijab. Talk to students about how in this scene, we don't really see the characters who are being unkind—they are just shadows—but we do see how they're hurting Asiya. Model self-questioning by asking yourself: *What feelings or misunderstandings might be causing this problem?* Then, share your thoughts about how this problem seems to stem from people not taking the time to understand someone whose culture is different from theirs and teasing based on differences.

> **SKILLS AND STANDARDS**
>
> **Comprehension Skill:**
> Identify problem and solution
>
> **CCSS:** RL.3.1, RL.3.3 • SL.3.1.A–C, SL.3.2, SL.3.6 • RL.4.1, RL.4.3 • SL.4.1.A–C, SL.4.2, SL.4.6
>
> **Social Justice:**
> JU.3-5.12 (I know when people are treated unfairly, and I can give examples of prejudiced words, pictures, and rules.)
>
> **CASEL:**
> **Social Awareness**
> - Recognize situational demands and opportunities
>
> **Responsible Decision-Making**
> - Anticipate and evaluate the consequences of one's actions

Circle Questions

Say to students: *In some stories, we know all the characters very well, and we understand what they think, need, and feel. In this story, however, the characters who cause the hurt feelings are not shown, and we don't know much about them. We may think that the cause of the problem is that they don't take the time to understand and welcome people's differences, and that may be true. But let's take a moment to think about why the author may have decided to keep them in the shadows. Why do you think the author did that?*

Afterwards, invite students to reflect by asking: *What ideas that were shared stand out most to you?*

Carryover Coaching

Use these additional prompts for one-on-one conferences.
- Look for moments of hurt feelings among characters.
- Think about what they're fighting about.
- Think about the characters and what you know about them. What do they want? What might they not understand?
- Put together what they're fighting over and what you know about them. Think about how that might explain why they're fighting.

SKILLS AND STANDARDS

Comprehension Skill:
Identify themes

CCSS: RL.3.2, RL.3.3, RL.3.4 • SL.3.1.A–C, SL.3.2, SL.3.6 • RL.4.2, RL.4.3, RL.4.4 • SL.4.1.A–C, SL.4.2, SL.4.6

Social Justice:
AC.3-5.16 (I pay attention to how people [including myself] are treated, and I try to treat others how I like to be treated.)

CASEL
Social Awareness
- Show concern for the feelings of others

Heartwork

Strategy: Readers pay close attention to when characters give advice.

As You Read . . .
- Notice when characters are giving advice to or supporting each other through a problem.
- Think about how the advice helps or hurts a character.
- Ask: *How might this advice help us learn a lesson from the story?*

Places to Pause

As you revisit the text, pause on the page that shows a close-up of Asiya in her blue hijab with clouds painted on it. Share with students that sometimes advice is given during conversations between characters. In this book, Mama's advice is woven across the pages as reminders. Focus on the bottom right part of the page that shows Mama's words of wisdom: *The first day of wearing hijab is important . . . It means being strong.* Pause to think about Mama's advice in this section. As you wonder aloud, ask yourself how being strong helps Asiya in her interactions with classmates throughout the day and what we all might learn from Mama's advice.

Circle Questions

Say to students: *In the story, we see bits of advice from Mama that Faizah remembers throughout the day. Let's give advice, too. Choose a character from the story—Faizah, Asiya, Asiya's friends, or the children who are teasing. Think about the challenges they're facing and their actions. What advice would you give them? Why?*

Afterwards, invite students to reflect by asking: *What did someone share that made you think, "Me too!"? What did someone share that helped you see something in a brand-new way?*

Carryover Coaching

Use these additional prompts for one-on-one conferences.
- Find a part in which a character seems to be offering advice about what to do or not do.
- Think about what that advice will lead to. Will that help the character or make things worse?
- Watch what happens next when the character follows or ignores the advice.
- Think about what you can learn in your everyday life based on the advice that was given.

Beyond the Book

Some of the most powerful and inspirational messages in this story can be found on the pages that show Mama's words echoing in the girls' minds as they experience challenges. Echoing words can be a wonderful tool to help center us during troubling times or motivate us when we need to persevere. In this activity, we invite students to develop mantras that can help them get through their own challenges and become the echoes that help them find peace, drive, and success. As you coach students and model with your own mantra, be sure to help them write words and phrases that are short, positive, and specific.

Say to students: *In the story* The Proudest Blue, *we see Faizah remembering her mama's words and using those words to help her when she felt upset. Many people use repeated words and phrases to feel better or motivate themselves. These repeated words that make us feel good are called* mantras. *We can say mantras to ourselves again and again to help us when we need a little boost. Today, we're going to make some mantras of our own.*

Share these steps to teach students how to make their own mantra:
- Think of times when you might benefit from some words of encouragement or belief.

SKILLS AND STANDARDS

CASEL:
Self-Management
- Manage one's emotions
- Identify and use stress-management strategies

- Close your eyes and imagine yourself in the moment. Ask yourself: *What words would make me feel good?* Or, *What words would cheer me on?* Turn those into an "I am" or "I can" statement.
- Write down those words and repeat them to yourself over and over.

Explain to students that mantras work best when we build them into habits and use them repeatedly. The repetition not only encourages us in the moment, but it can also change the ways we view ourselves and our mindsets.

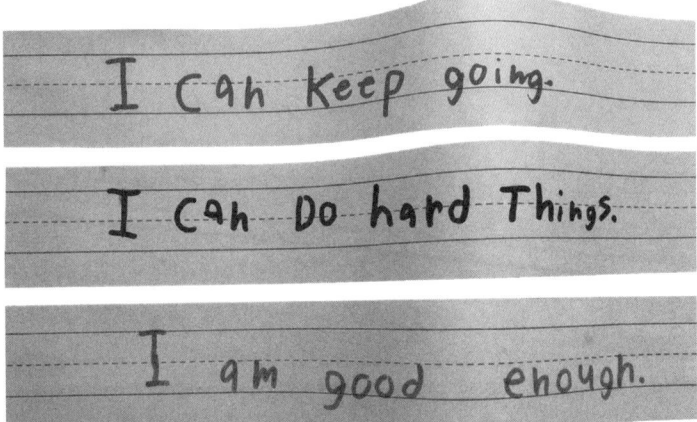

Students come up with their own mantras to cheer them on.

A Few More Favorites

The Day You Begin
by Jacqueline Woodson

Oliver Button Is a Sissy
by Tomie DePaola

SEPARATE IS NEVER EQUAL:

Sylvia Mendez and Her Family's Fight for Desegregation

Written and illustrated by Duncan Tonatiuh
Grades 4–5 / Biography / #OwnVoices

A Bit About the Book

As we turn the pages of this empowering book, we learn the true story of Sylvia Mendez and her family. A child in the 1940s, Sylvia loved to learn. But due to unfair laws of segregation based on race or national origin, Sylvia and her brothers were unable to attend the school in their town because of their identity. Facing many challenges, Sylvia and her family were determined to make a change. With the support and sacrifices of her family, community, and numerous organizations, Sylvia's dream of attending a desegregated school finally came true. Be sure to read the author's note in the back of the book for more details on this true story.

 **Identity**

Strategy: Readers of biographies consider how subjects can be treated unfairly because of how they look or where they are from.

As You Read . . .
- Look closely at the pictures.
- Think about the ways the subject is portrayed in comparison to the other people in the book.
- Pause in the places in which the subject's appearance or identity is compared to those of others.
- Ask: *How does the subject's identity impact the way in which others treat her?*

Places to Pause

Pause on the page after Aunt Soledad takes Sylvia, her brothers, and her cousins to the neighborhood school to enroll them. Share what you notice about how the school's secretary responds to the family and how she allows the cousins to attend the school, but not Sylvia or her brothers. Point to the page in which Sylvia looks at herself and compares her skin and hair to her cousins'. Model your thinking about how Sylvia is treated unfairly because of how she looks compared to her cousins, even though they are from the same family and live in the same town.

Circle Questions

Say to students: *Let's reflect on Sylvia's experience when she was not allowed to attend the school because of her skin and hair, even though her cousins were*

SKILLS AND STANDARDS

Comprehension Skill:
Analyze subject

CCSS: RI.4.2, RI.4.3, RI.4.7, RI.4.8 • SL.4.1, SL.4.4 • RI.5.2, RI.5.3, RI.5.7, RI.5.8 • SL.5.1, SL.5.4

Social Justice:
JU.3-5.14 (I know that life is easier for some people and harder for others based on who they are and where they were born.)

CASEL:
Self-Awareness
- Integrate personal and social identities
- Link feelings, values, and thoughts
- Examine prejudices and biases

Responsible Decision-Making
- Evaluate personal, interpersonal, community, and institutional impacts

Social Awareness
- Identify diverse social norms, including unjust ones
- Understand the influences of organizations and systems on behavior

permitted to attend. Where else in stories, history, or your own experiences have you observed something similar? Share your thoughts or reflections.

Afterwards, invite students to reflect by saying: *Think about what your classmates shared. Write down something that was said that might be new learning for you.*

Carryover Coaching
Use these additional prompts for one-on-one conferences.
- Pause in the parts that show the subject's interactions with others.
- Make connections between the interactions and the subject's physical appearance.

> **SKILLS AND STANDARDS**
>
> **Comprehension Skill:** Consider subject/character's perspective
>
> **CCSS:** RI.4.2, RI.4.3, RI.4.7, RI.4.8 • SL.4.1, SL.4.4 • RI.5.2, RI.5.3, RI.5.7, RI.5.8 • SL.5.1, SL.5.4
>
> **Social Justice:**
> JU.3-5.13 (I know that words, behaviors, rules, and laws that treat people unfairly based on their group identities cause real harm.)
>
> **CASEL:**
> Social Awareness
> • Identify diverse social norms, including unjust ones
>
> Responsible Decision-Making
> • Identify solutions for personal and social problems
> • Evaluate personal, interpersonal, community, and institutional impacts

Harm and Healing

Strategy: Readers of biographies keep track of unfair actions that happen over time.

As You Read . . .
- Pause on the moments when the subject faces unfairness.
- List these moments as they happen over time in the story.
- Ask: *How did all these events impact this person?*

Places to Pause
Pause on the pages that show when Sylvia, her family, and those who share in her identity face unfair treatment. Share your thinking about how this happens over time and create a timeline of those moments on chart paper. Be sure to emphasize aloud that many of the moments took place over several years.

Circle Questions
Say to students: *We notice throughout the story how Sylvia and her community faced unfair treatment on many different occasions across time. Think about and write down an action you would take to support Sylvia. Share this aloud.*

Afterwards, invite students to reflect by asking: *What is something new you heard from your classmates as they shared? Write down a goal you will set for yourself to help others when you see someone else being treated unfairly inside or outside of school.*

Carryover Coaching
Use these additional prompts for one-on-one conferences.
- Read through the story.
- Take notice of the subject's experience.
- Tell the subject's experiences across the pages.

 **Heartwork**

Strategy: Readers of biographies recognize that subjects can work together to overcome obstacles.

As You Read...
- Notice the actions of the people working together.
- Write down the results from the actions the people took together.

Places to Pause
Reflect on the pages in which we see the work of numerous people coming together to support the end of segregated schooling. Share out loud what you notice about various people, such as Mr. Marcus in his role as the family's lawyer, Sylvia's father informing and supporting other Mexican American families, Sylvia's mother helping on the farm while her father fought for change, and the community and other leagues and associations of various identity groups joining to support the family. Think aloud about how the actions of various people working together led to greater change against unfair treatments.

Circle Questions
Say to students: *As we read the story, we notice that Sylvia and her family worked hard to change the laws. But working together with and receiving support from the larger community gave them a boost in their fight against unfair treatment. Why was this helpful for Sylvia and other children and families just like her? Share your reflections.*

Afterwards, invite students to reflect by saying: *Pause and reflect on a moment when you worked with others to help make a positive change or fight against unfair treatment. Write down your reflections and share.*

Carryover Coaching
Use these additional prompts for one-on-one conferences.
- List what you know about the experiences the subject faced.
- Make connections to the actions of the subject and others in response to these experiences.
- Draw upon these connections to deepen your understanding.

SKILLS AND STANDARDS

Comprehension Skill:
Identify problem and solution

CCSS: RI.4.2, RI.4.3, RI.4.7, RI.4.8 • SL.4.1, SL.4.4 • RI.5.2, RI.5.3, RI.5.7, RI.5.8 • SL.5.1, SL.5.4

Social Justice:
JU.3-5.15 (I know about the actions of people and groups who have worked throughout history to bring more justice and fairness to the world.)

CASEL:
Responsible Decision-Making
- Identify solutions for personal and social problems
- Reflect on one's role to promote personal, family, and community well-being

Relationship Skills
- Resolve conflicts constructively
- Practice teamwork and collaborative problem-solving
- Seek and offer support and help when needed
- Stand up for the rights of others

SKILLS AND STANDARDS

CASEL:

Responsible Decision-Making
- Reflect on one's role to promote personal, family, and community well-being

Relationship Skills
- Stand up for the rights of others
- Practice teamwork and collaborative problem-solving
- Seek and offer support and help when needed

Beyond the Book

After reading this powerful story of unity and justice, make note of the ways Sylvia, her family, and her community came together to take action and make sacrifices to create better opportunities for themselves and for future generations to come. As a class, research action projects that classroom communities around the nation are taking part in. With your students, brainstorm ways your class or school can come together as a community to participate in taking action to make positive change. You can reach out to your school leadership team for a change in the school or to the broader community through the local municipality, parks department, and so on. Positive changes can include cleaning up a playground or park, organizing a food or clothing drive, creating stories for classroom libraries within the school, and so on. Be sure to emphasize the importance of working together to bring positive change, no matter how big or small.

People who received unfair treatment and did something about it.

A Few More Favorites

Let the Children March by Monica Clark-Robinson

Someday Is Now by Olugbemisola Rhuday-Perkovich

THE CASE FOR LOVING:
The Fight for Interracial Marriage

Written by Selina Alko / Illustrated by Sean Qualls and Selina Alko
Grades 4–5 / Biography / #OwnVoices

A Bit About the Book
This engaging book tells the true story of the Lovings. Mildred and Richard met in the 1950s in their small town in Virginia. They fell in love and decided to get married. However, because Mildred is a woman of color and Richard is a White man, the state laws did not recognize their marriage as legal. Through many hardships and hurdles, Mildred and Richard fought to keep their love and their family together. They even had to move their family away from home. The fight for justice did not end there, and their case went to the Supreme Court. The court ordered Virginia's unfair laws to be changed, and the Lovings were able to return home and live in union and love forever!

 **Identity**

Strategy: Readers of biographies know that relationships can be formed across different identities.

As You Read . . .
- Look closely at the pictures.
- Think about the ways the subjects differ from each other.
- Take note when the subjects have positive interactions.
- Ask: *How do the subjects' interactions impact their relationship?*

Places to Pause
Read from the beginning of the story and pause on the page in which Richard proposes to Mildred. Share your thoughts about what you noticed about how their relationship grew over the past few pages. Create a chart that lists the differences between Mildred and Richard, and then list the things they have in common (e.g., their care and love for each other, living in the same town). Think aloud about how although the two subjects were different from each other, they were still able to develop a growing and caring bond.

Circle Questions
Say to students: *Let's reflect on the things we know about Richard and Mildred. What things can we list about their identities? Think about how the two of them were able to care for and love each other despite their differences. Write down your thoughts or reflections.*

Afterwards, invite students to reflect by saying: *Think about how we can develop connections with and care for other people, regardless of our*

SKILLS AND STANDARDS

Comprehension Skill:
Analyze subjects' relationships

CCSS: RL.4.1, RL.4.3 • RI.4.1 • SL.4.1, SL.4.2, SL.4.6 • RL.5.1, RL.5.3 • RI.5.1 • SL.5.1, SL.5.2, SL.5.6

Social Justice:
DI.3-5.9 (I feel connected to other people and know how to talk, work, and play with others even when we are different or when we disagree.)

CASEL:

Relationship Skills
- Develop positive relationships
- Resist negative social pressure

Self-Awareness
- Integrate personal and social identities
- Identify personal, cultural, and linguistic assets

Read-Alouds With Heart: Grades 3–5 • 115

differences. *Think about your personal connections. Is there a person with whom you have a bond even though you're different from each other? Share aloud.*

Carryover Coaching

Use these additional prompts for one-on-one conferences.

- Pause in the places that show the subjects interacting with each other.
- Take notice of the subjects' identities and their similarities and differences.
- Ask: *What connection do the subjects have that goes beyond their differences?*

SKILLS AND STANDARDS

Comprehension Skill:
Consider subjects' perspectives

CCSS: RL.4.1, RL.4.3 • RI.4.1 • SL.4.1, SL.4.2, SL.4.6 • RL.5.1, RL.5.3 • RI.5.1 • SL.5.1, SL.5.2, SL.5.6

Social Justice:
JU.3-5.12 (I know when people are treated unfairly, and I can give examples of prejudiced words, pictures, and rules.)

CASEL:
Social Awareness
- Identify diverse social norms, including unjust ones
- Understand the influences of organizations and systems on behavior

Responsible Decision-Making
- Evaluate personal, interpersonal, community, and institutional impacts

Harm and Healing

Strategy: Readers of biographies analyze the ways people are treated unfairly across all types of identities.

As You Read . . .
- Make note of the subjects' identities.
- Pause on the moments when the subjects face unfairness.
- Reflect on the causes of these unfair treatments.

Places to Pause

Pause across the pages to quickly note the moments when Mildred and Richard, who have differences in their identities, both face unfair treatment. Share your thinking about how this unfair treatment is happening to both of them, based on the differences in their identities.

Circle Questions

Say to students: *We notice throughout the story that Mildred and Richard are left to deal with the results of unfair treatments and rules. Think and write about other unfair rules you have read about in other stories. Share these aloud.*

Afterwards, invite students to reflect by asking: *What do you think are some unfair or unjust rules that exist today? Write how you would work to change those rules and the actions you can take. Share aloud.*

Carryover Coaching

Use these additional prompts for one-on-one conferences.

- Reread through the story.
- Take notice of the subjects' experiences with unfair treatment.
- Draw a connection between the subjects' identities and the unfair treatment.

 **Heartwork**

Strategy: Readers of biographies learn about the joy that can come after overcoming hardships together.

As You Read . . .
- Notice the actions of the subjects working together to overcome hardships.
- Write about the results of the actions the subjects took together.
- Reflect on the subjects' expressions after achieving those results.

Places to Pause
Pause and reflect on the last two pages of the story, in which the author writes "they were free at last" and "happily and (legally) ever after!" Share your reflections about how the Lovings had to overcome many hardships and fight for justice. Their case went all the way up to the Supreme Court, which finally ruled that their marriage was legal. Model how you notice the expressions on the characters' faces thereafter. Think aloud about the joy they felt at being married (legally) and being able to move back to Virginia to raise their children in their hometown.

Circle Questions
Say to students: *We read about the hardships the Lovings faced throughout the story. After overcoming the challenges, we see their expressions of joy. What are the reasons the Lovings might feel this way? What are some other emotions we can use to describe their feelings? Share your reflections.*

Afterwards, invite students to reflect by saying: *Let's share in the feeling that Mildred and Richard felt after overcoming their challenges. Think about a time when you felt joy after overcoming a hardship. Write down your reflections and share.*

Carryover Coaching
Use these additional prompts for one-on-one conferences.
- List what you know about the challenges the subjects faced.
- Take notice of the subjects' feelings after overcoming the challenges.
- Write down your own understandings and connections.

SKILLS AND STANDARDS

Comprehension Skill:
Identify problem and solution

CCSS: RL.4.1, RL.4.3 • RI.4.1 • SL.4.1, SL.4.2, SL.4.6 • RL.5.1, RL.5.3 • RI.5.1 • SL.5.1, SL.5.2, SL.5.6

Social Justice:
JU.3-5.15 (I know about the actions of people and groups who have worked throughout history to bring more justice and fairness to the world.)

CASEL:
Responsible Decision-Making
- Identify solutions for personal and social problems
- Reflect on one's role to promote personal, family, and community well-being

Relationship Skills
- Resolve conflicts constructively
- Practice teamwork and collaborative problem-solving
- Seek and offer support and help when needed
- Stand up for the rights of others

SKILLS AND STANDARDS

CASEL:
Self-Management
- Manage one's emotions
- Identify and use stress-management strategies

📖 Beyond the Book

We often share in the feelings of the subjects or characters we read about in books. As we read this story about love and justice, we see the Loving family overcome many obstacles. But certain situations along their journey may have caused us to feel frustration and upset at the injustices the family faced.

Invite students to practice breathing strategies to bring calmness and grounding during these moments. Have them place their hands on their knees, with palms facing up or down. Encourage them to take a breath in through their nose and gently exhale out of their mouth. Repeat this a few times. Next, tell students as they inhale to think of those difficult feelings that might arise and then to release those feelings as they exhale. Repeat this a few times. Remind students they can use this breathing strategy any time these feelings arise.

Students practice breathing strategies as a way to cope with feelings of frustration or upset.

A Few More Favorites

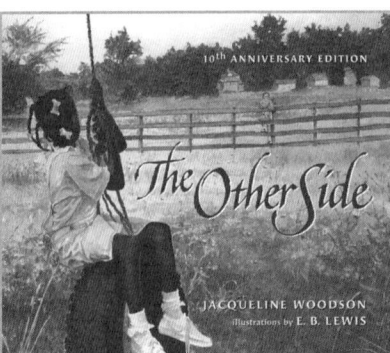

The Other Side
by Jacqueline Woodson

Two Grooms on a Cake: The Story of America's First Gay Wedding
by Rob Sanders

WATERCRESS

Written by Andrea Wang / Illustrated by Jason Chin
Grades 4–5 / Realistic Fiction / #OwnVoices

A Bit About the Book
In *Watercress*, we follow one girl's journey toward understanding how her life and her family's history come together. At the beginning of the story, we meet a young girl embarrassed by her family's circumstances. As she and her family trudge through mud and muck at the side of the road to gather watercress, she prays no one spots her. Her disgust at how her family came to acquire their free meal carries into the evening—until her mother shares a piece of her personal history that changes the girl's feelings. This story of reflection and revelation is sure to pull on your heartstrings!

 ## Identity

Strategy: Readers know that people's experiences shape who they are or how they think.

As You Read . . .
- Look for experiences that happen throughout the story.
- Look for the moment when a character shares about her past.
- Think about the emotions that character felt during that past experience.
- Ask: *How has this experience shaped this character? How does this experience connect to why the character acts or thinks the way she does or believes what she believes?*

Places to Pause
Pause on the page that shows the girl thinking that "free is bad." Think aloud about how in her own experiences, she connects "free" to being teased or feeling different. Because of those experiences, she feels ashamed about the watercress and her family. Share your thoughts on how her experiences have led to the way she thinks.

* Note: We know the girl's thinking will change later in the story. You may want to revisit this think-aloud through the lens of the girl's new understanding, which changes her initial thinking.

Circle Questions
Say to students: *Think about the experiences of the characters across the story. Choose one experience that stands out most to you. Share how that experience has helped you understand something about that character.* Offer this sentence stem to help students: "Because ____ experienced ____, I understood that she (was/thought/believed) ____."

SKILLS AND STANDARDS

Comprehension Skills:
Analyze character; consider character's perspective

CCSS: RL.4.1, RL.4.3 • SL.4.1.A–C, SL.4.2, SL.4.6 • RL.5.1 • SL.5.1.A–C, SL.5.2, SL.5.6

Social Justice:
DI.3-5.10 (I know that the way groups of people are treated today, and the way they have been treated in the past, is a part of what makes them who they are.)

CASEL:
Social Awareness
- Take others' perspectives
- Demonstrate empathy and compassion

Afterwards, invite students to reflect by asking: *What did someone share that made you think, "Me too!"? What did someone share that helped you see something in a brand-new way?*

Carryover Coaching
Use these additional prompts for one-on-one conferences.
- Look for experiences tied to big feelings.
- Think about moments when characters share past experiences.
- Pay close attention to the character's reaction here. How does this affect her?
- Put the experience and her action/belief together.

SKILLS AND STANDARDS

Comprehension Skill:
Identify theme

CCSS: RL.4.1, RL.4.2 • SL.4.1.A–C, SL.4.2, SL.4.6 • RL.5.1, RL.5.2, RL.5.6 • SL.5.1.A–C, SL.5.2, SL.5.6

Social Justice:
JU.3-5.15 (I know about the actions of people and groups who have worked throughout history to bring more justice and fairness to the world.)

CASEL:
Social Awareness
- Recognize situational demands and opportunities

Responsible Decision-Making
- Reflect on one's role to promote personal, family, and community well-being
- Evaluate personal, interpersonal, community, and institutional impacts

Harm and Healing

Strategy: Readers look for lessons they can learn from books by looking for moments when there may be a change of heart or a new understanding.

As You Read . . .
- Look for a moment when the character's thinking or feelings about something changed completely.
- Notice what brought about that change. What did the character learn, see, or begin to understand?
- Ask: *What did the lesson the character learned teach us all?*

Places to Pause
Pause on the page that shows the girl holding the photograph of her mom's family and talking about feeling ashamed. Think aloud about how we see a shift from the girl feeling ashamed of her family to her feeling ashamed of herself. While the feeling itself didn't change, its direction did. Talk about how the mom sharing the memory of her own brother triggered this shift and how the girl may have learned to see her family's actions differently now that she saw what poverty and starvation cost her mom's family. Then, share how you might turn this lesson the girl learned into a universal lesson for all of us. You can frame this in many different ways. For example, we can learn to be grateful for what we have. Another lesson could be how important it is to learn about our families' stories to understand them and ourselves.

Circle Questions
Read aloud the author's note. Invite students to reflect on the author's personal experiences and how they shaped the book. Say to students: *Think about what may have driven the author to write this story. How do you think her own experiences connected to the lessons we can learn from her storytelling?* Offer this sentence stem to students: "When I heard that she ____, I understood that she wanted to teach people ____."

Afterwards, invite students to reflect by asking: *What thoughts that were shared stood out most to you? Which do you connect to?*

Carryover Coaching

Use these additional prompts for one-on-one conferences.
- Look for a shift in feeling in the book.
- Look for parts in which a character acts in a way you wouldn't expect.
- Revisit the parts that happened right before the change.
- Consider how this event changed the character's mind.
- Ask: *What can we learn from how the character changed?*

Strategy: Readers know that emotions can sometimes be layered and even conflicting. Moments of conflicting emotion are often windows into important parts of a story.

As You Read . . .
- Pause during a moment of big feelings. Name the clear emotion that pops out first.
- Take a moment to ask yourself if there is something else there, too. You might discover another feeling hiding underneath by paying attention to what characters are thinking of or remembering.
- Ask: *What does this help me understand?*

Places to Pause

Pause on the page that shows the girl taking a bite of the watercress and her mom holding the picture of her family in China. Zoom in on the mother. Think aloud how the mom might be feeling at this moment. Your think-aloud might sound something like this: *Mom is happy to share this free and delicious meal that is connected to her childhood with her own children, and yet remembering her brother adds a layer of sadness.* Explain to students that when we feel like this, it is called *bittersweet*—it's a moment when you feel happy about one thing but sad about another. Seeing this layered feeling can help us understand why the mother doesn't talk about her life in China much. It must be hard to remember the pain of that time.

Circle Questions

For this circle, we offer two parts of the story you might decide to revisit. Choose the one you think your students will understand or connect with most.

Choice 1: Go back to the part in which the girl says, "Free is bad." Spend a moment closely studying the words and pictures, highlighting the pointing and the standing alone.

SKILLS AND STANDARDS

Comprehension Skills: Analyze character; determine importance

CCSS: RL.4.1, RL.4.3 • SL.4.1.A-C, SL.4.2, SL.4.6 • RL.5.1 • SL.5.1.A-C, SL.5.2, SL.5.6

Social Justice:
DI.3-5.10 (I know that the way people are treated today, and the way they have been treated in the past, is part of what makes them who they are.)

CASEL:
Self-Awareness
- Identify one's emotions
- Demonstrate honesty and integrity
- Link feelings, values, and thoughts

Social Awareness
- Take others' perspectives
- Recognize strengths in others

Choice 2: Go back to the four pages that show the family in the ditch as a car drives by and then the girl's brother holding the watercress over her head. Spend a moment revisiting the body language of the characters and the verb choice that describe the characters' actions.

Whichever part you decided to revisit, invite students to look for more than one feeling in this section. Say: *Let's go back to this part of the story. Take a moment to name a couple of feelings happening here. Then, as we hear the feelings named in our circle, we can think about how the layers of different feelings help us understand more about the girl.* Offer this sentence stem to students: "I think she feels ____ and ____." On chart paper, record the feelings named in the circle.

Afterwards, invite students to reflect by asking: *What do the new feelings that were named here help you understand about the girl?*

Carryover Coaching

Use these additional prompts for one-on-one conferences.
- Pay close attention to what the character is thinking about at a particular moment.
- Ask: *What else is happening that might cause another feeling?*
- Consider how a new feeling might explain something about what the character is doing or what is going on.

SKILLS AND STANDARDS

CASEL:
Self-Awareness
- Identify one's emotions
- Link feelings, values, and thoughts

Beyond the Book

Watercress brings to the surface an emotion that is felt by all, rarely spoken, and should be addressed—shame. Feeling shame is part of the human experience, and yet most of us do everything in our power to hide it like a dirty secret. In this activity, we hope to spend a few sessions helping students learn the difference between feeling guilty and feeling shame, understand that they are not alone in these feelings, and have strategies that can help them move forward. Much of this work is inspired by our mentor and guide, Brené Brown.

Say to students: *In our story, the main character tells us that she felt ashamed. At first, she was ashamed of her family and how they got their clothes, furniture, and food. Later, she switches to feeling ashamed of herself. When we experience this type of feeling, it is important to acknowledge whether it is showing up as guilt or shame. Let's explore the differences and what we can do when we feel shame.*

Take a moment to compare shame and guilt. Highlight that guilt is feeling bad about *something* you've done while shame is feeling bad about *who* you are. Shame sends the "I'm bad or not enough" message, while guilt is focused on a poor choice or an action. Offer an example of what shame and guilt sound like and then have students turn and talk to a partner to see if they can list more examples. For example, shame is when you yell at your brother and you later say, "I'm so mean. I'm the worst brother ever." Guilt is when you yell at your brother and later say, "I shouldn't have yelled. That was a mean thing to do."

Tell students that while we all feel shame sometimes, it's important to acknowledge when we're feeling shame and then do something to move out of it. The steps below can act as a guide to help students recognize and respond.

1. **Listen for your language.** "I am" statements often equal shame.
2. **Name it.** Change your self-talk.
3. **Share.** Find someone you trust and tell them what happened. When we share, we no longer feel alone, and sometimes our friends share their own moments of shame with us, too.

Note: A wonderful complementary text that can help students explore this emotion further is *A Kid's Book About Shame,* by Jamie Letourneau. (This whole series is another fantastic resource.)

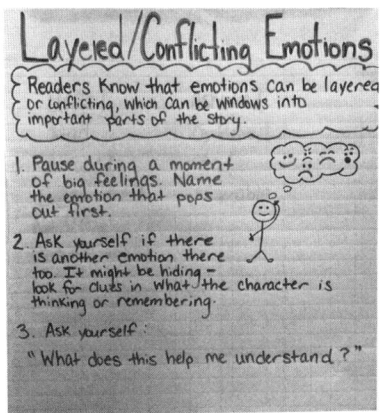 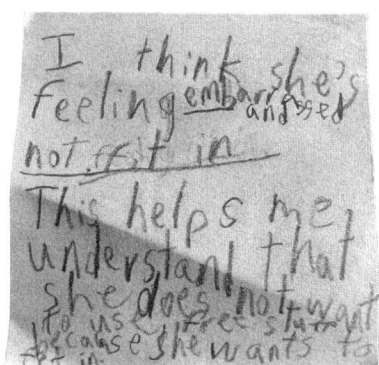 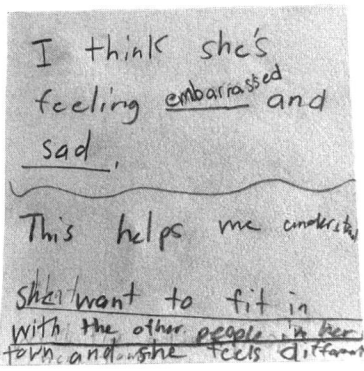

Students reflect on the character's emotions to help them understand her better.

A Few More Favorites

A Different Pond
by Bao Phi

A Bike Like Sergio's
by Maribeth Boelts

WE ARE WATER PROTECTORS

Written by Carole Lindstrom / Illustrated by Michaela Goade
Grades 3–5 / Narrative Nonfiction / #OwnVoices

A Bit About the Book

In this gorgeous picture book, Carole Lindstrom uses a young girl to tell the story of her tribe's Seven Fires Prophecy, a warning against the mistreatment of Earth and our water. Faced with the fact that her ancestor's cautionary tale is becoming a reality, she urges us to fight against the "black snake" pipelines that have come to poison all living things. Lindstrom uses her voice to stand up for environmental justice. The lyrical lines of this book read like a song, but the text's message stays with you and rallies like a war cry.

Note: Be sure to read the last page, "More on Water Protectors," to offer students background on the Indigenous People's fight for clean land and water.

SKILLS AND STANDARDS

Comprehension Skill:
Analyze character

CCSS: RL.3.1, RL.3.3 • RI.3.1 • SL.3.1.A–C, SL.3.2, SL.3.6 • RL.4.1, RL.4.3 • RI.4.1 • SL.4.1.A, B, D; SL.4.2; SL.4.6 • RL.5.1, RL.5.3 • RI.5.1 • SL.5.1.A, B, D; SL.5.2; SL.5.6

Social Justice:
JU.3-5.14 (I know that life is easier for some people and harder for others based on who they are and where they were born.)

CASEL:
Social Awareness
• Take others' perspectives
• Recognize strengths in others

Identity

Strategy: Readers know that people's identities are formed by the stories of their culture and family. They pay attention to these stories and ask themselves how they fit the characters.

As You Read . . .

- Notice when a character is sharing a tradition or story from their family or culture.
- Ask: *What am I learning about this person's culture from this story? What am I learning about her identity? How does this explain what may be important to her?*
- Consider how the tradition or story explains something the person believes, does, or values.

Places to Pause

Pause on the page that shows the "black snake" pipeline against the red background. Thinking aloud, talk about how the stories that the grandmother shares make the girl ready to be a protector and fighter.

Circle Questions

Say to students: *Think about the stories the girl heard about her people and the water. How might these stories have helped make her who she is?*

Afterwards, invite students to reflect by asking: *What ideas that were shared stand out most to you?*

Carryover Coaching

Use these additional prompts for one-on-one conferences.
- Think about the family members of the characters in their book.
- Ask if the characters have shared any family stories or traditions.
- Think about how those stories and traditions make the character who they are and act the way they do.

 Harm and Healing

Strategy: Readers know that a problem can affect more than just one person or character. They consider who the problem affects and how the problem affects them.

As You Read . . .
- Name a problem of the main character.
- Look at the people around that character—friends, family, community members, and so on.
- Think about how the character's problem affects others.

Places to Pause

Pause on the pages that show the animals in the jungle and by the mountains. Model your thinking to show how the problem of the "black snake" pipeline is affecting people and animals. Share your thinking about how people's choices have an impact on the lives of those who have no say.

Circle Questions

Say to students: *Think about the pipeline the little girl calls the "black snake" in this story. Who will be affected by that pipeline? How will they be affected? What does that make you think?*

Afterwards, invite students to reflect by asking: *What do you now wonder about or want to learn more about?*

Carryover Coaching

Use these additional prompts for one-on-one conferences.
- Think about the problems you have seen in the book.
- Notice who is being affected by the problem now.
- Think about who else might be affected.
- Consider how the problem is hurting this person.

SKILLS AND STANDARDS

Comprehension Skill:
Identify problem and solution

CCSS: RL.3.1, RL.3.3 • RI.3.1 • SL.3.1.A–C, SL.3.2, SL.3.6 • RL.4.1, RL.4.3 • RI.4.1 • SL.4.1.A–C, SL.4.2, SL.4.6 • RL.5.1, RL.5.3 • RI.5.1 • SL.5.1.A–C, SL.5.2, SL.5.6

Social Justice:
JU.3-5.13 (I know that words, behaviors, rules, and laws that treat people unfairly based on their group identities cause real harm.)

CASEL:
Responsible Decision-Making
- Reflect on one's role to promote personal, family, and community well-being
- Evaluate personal, interpersonal, community, and institutional impacts

SKILLS AND STANDARDS

Comprehension Skills: Make inferences; analyze word choice

CCSS: RL.3.3, RL.3.4 • SL.3.1.A–C, SL.3.2, SL.3.6 • RL.4.3, RL.4.4 • SL.4.1.A–C, SL.4.2, SL.4.6 • RL.5.3, RL.5.4 • SL.5.1.A–C, SL.5.2, SL.5.6

Social Justice:
JU.3-5.13 (I know that words, behaviors, rules, and laws that treat people unfairly based on their group identities cause real harm.)

CASEL:

Self-Awareness
- Identify one's emotions
- Demonstrate honesty and integrity
- Link feelings, values, and thoughts

Social Awareness
- Take others' perspectives
- Recognize strengths in others

Heartwork

Strategy: Readers share a character's heart and feelings by thinking about the words she uses.

As You Read . . .
- Notice the words the character says.
- Think about the power and feeling behind the words.
- Put yourself into the character's place to feel those same feelings.

Places to Pause
Pause on the page that shows the little girl holding her fist up in the air with her hair flowing behind her. Model thinking about the strength of her words. Focus on the words *courage* and *must* and what they say about the strength of her emotions. Talk through how you can feel those emotions in your own heart as you read the girl's words and think about her life.

Circle Questions
On chart paper, write some of your favorite lines from the text or invite students to choose their favorite lines to be recorded. Ask students: *What do those words mean in this story? What do they say about how the character feels? What feelings do you feel along with her?*

Afterwards, invite students to reflect by asking: *What did someone share that made you think, "Me too!"? What did someone share that helped you see something in a brand-new way?*

Carryover Coaching
Use these additional prompts for one-on-one conferences.
- Find a part in which the character is talking to someone else or even to herself.
- Think about what is happening and the character's words.
- Notice how heavy or light the words feel.
- Think: *When you've heard or used words like that, what did you feel? What must the character be feeling?*
- Place the character's heart in you own. What are you feeling?

Beyond the Book

This activity is a celebratory circle prompt. One aspect of our study is dedicated to acknowledging family and cultural traditions. Even the smallest traditions can help shape us and add to our identities. By sharing a tradition from our homes, we celebrate one another and add layers of getting to know one another even more intimately.

Say to students: *Think about a tradition that is part of your home life. Traditions are formed in many different ways. They might be tied to a holiday, a part of your family's culture, or even a little routine that your family has developed. Is there a tradition you'd like to share with us? What is your tradition and what do you enjoy about it?*

SKILLS AND STANDARDS

CASEL:
Self-Awareness
- Integrate personal and social identities
- Identify personal, cultural, and linguistic assets

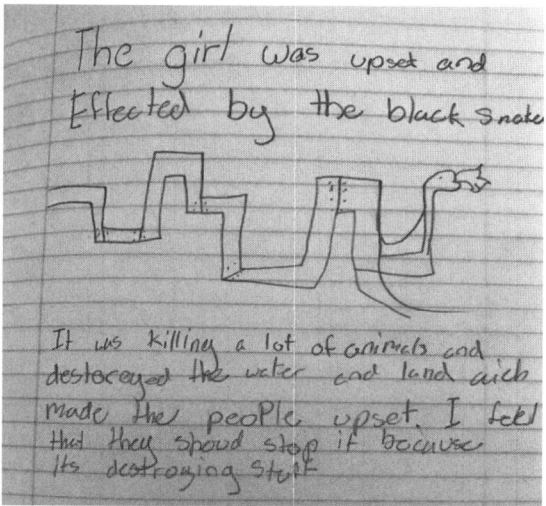

A student reflects on how the "black snake" pipeline affects people and animals.

A Few More Favorites

Greta and the Giants: Inspired by Greta Thunberg's Stand to Save the World
by Zoë Tucker

Our World Out of Balance: Understanding Climate Change and What We Can Do
by Andrea Minoglio

YOUR NAME IS A SONG

Written by Jamilah Thompkins-Bigelow / Illustrated by Luisa Uribe
Grades 3–4 / Fiction / #OwnVoices

A Bit About the Book

This beautiful story shines light on the significance of honoring and sharing our names. As we turn the pages, we read about a little girl who tells her mother about her frustrations from school when her teacher and her classmates were unable to pronounce her name. Be sure to look at the Glossary of Names Featured in the Story at the end of the book. A video of the author pronouncing the names in the story is also available, serving as a wonderful resource to review before beginning the read-aloud.

SKILLS AND STANDARDS

Comprehension Skill:
Analyze character interactions

CCSS: RL.3.1, RL.3.3, RL.3.4 • SL.3.1, SL.3.4 • RL.4.2, RL.4.3, RL.4.4 • SL.4.1, SL.4.4

Social Justice:
ID.3-5.4 (I can feel good about my identity without making someone else feel badly about who they are.)

CASEL:
Self-Awareness
- Integrate personal and social identities
- Identify personal, cultural, and linguistic assets
- Examine prejudices and biases

Social Awareness
- Identify diverse social norms, including unjust ones

 ## Identity

Strategy: Readers look for changes in the characters by noticing changes in the way they interact and talk with one another.

As You Read . . .
- Pause in parts that display the dialogue between the character and her family.
- Ask: *What do the characters express to one another?*
- Name how the characters respond or change through the conversations.

Places to Pause

Pause after the page in which the character's mother tells her that names come from the sky. Think aloud as you make connections between how the girl felt about her name and identity and the ways her mother responds.

Circle Questions

Say to students: *Let's think back to all the ways the character's mother responds to her when she shares her struggles in school with her name and identity. Why do you think her mother tells her to sing names like a song? What are some of the words of wisdom she shares with her daughter to help her communicate about her identity with others? How do you think this impacted the girl's feelings about herself and her name?*

Afterwards, invite students to reflect by saying: *Think about a time when you felt supported by someone as you faced a challenge about yourself and/or your identity.*

Carryover Coaching

Use these additional prompts for one-on-one conferences.
- Think about how the character is supported in learning how to communicate with others about her identity.
- Consider how our communicating with respect and knowledge builds bridges between the similarities and differences in our identities.

Harm and Healing

Strategy: Readers notice how other characters react when someone shares a belief or takes a stand.

As You Read . . .
- Notice when the character takes an action to stand against bias and misunderstanding.
- Ask: *What happened right before this moment? What happened during it? What happened after?*
- Pay attention to how the characters respond to this moment.

Places to Pause
Pause after the page in which the character shares with her teacher and classmates that names are songs and begins to sing their names. Take notice of the teacher's reaction as well as her classmates' reactions. Share what you notice about the character's reaction to this moment.

Circle Questions
Ask students: *What did you notice the girl do when the teacher responded to her by huffing, "Names are not songs"?*

Afterwards, invite students to reflect by saying: *Write about a time when you observed bias or misunderstanding or took a stand against it. What did that moment feel like? What happened as a result of those actions?*

Carryover Coaching
Use these additional prompts for one-on-one conferences.
- Look at the impact that biases and misunderstandings have on the character's feelings.
- Take note of the character's actions to find a solution for this problem.
- Think about the cause and effect of the character's actions to solve this problem.

SKILLS AND STANDARDS

Comprehension Skill: Identify actions and consequences

CCSS: RL.3.1, RL.3.3, RL.3.4 • SL.3.1, SL.3.4 • RL.4.2, RL.4.3, RL.4.4 • SL.4.1, SL.4.4

Social Justice:
AC.3-5.17 (I know it's important for me to stand up for myself and for others, and I know how to get help if I need ideas on how to do this.)

CASEL:
Responsible Decision-Making
- Identify solutions for personal and social problems
- Reflect on one's role to promote personal, family, and community well-being

Relationship Skills
- Resolve conflicts constructively
- Seek or offer support and help when needed

SKILLS AND STANDARDS

Comprehension Skill:
Analyze change in character

CCSS: RL.3.1, RL.3.3, RL.3.4 • SL.3.1, SL.3.4 • RL.4.2, RL.4.3, RL.4.4 • SL.4.1, SL.4.4

Social Justice:
AC.3-5.18 (I know some ways to interfere if someone is being hurtful or unfair, and I will do my part to show respect even if I disagree with someone's words or behavior.)

CASEL:
Self-Management
- Show the courage to take initiative
- Demonstrate personal and collective agency

Self-Awareness
- Show leadership in groups
- Stand up for the rights of others

 Heartwork

Strategy: Readers consider how characters can connect their actions to outcomes.

As You Read . . .
- Think about the moments when the character recognized her responsibility in actions and outcomes.
- Write down the actions the character took to stand up for something she believed in.

Places to Pause
Pause on the page in which Ms. Anderson's frown turns to a smile as the character's classmates ask her to sing their names, too. Model your reflections by taking notice of the character's expressions after she took this action. Think aloud about the connections between the characters' expressions and their thoughts and feelings.

Circle Questions
Say to students: *Take a moment to connect to the character when she sings her name aloud and when everyone joined in to sing it, too. Sit with the feelings the girl must be feeling at this moment. Connect with the character by thinking of a time when you felt the same way. Was it after a moment of taking action? Share with the class.*

Afterwards, invite students to reflect by saying: *What did someone share that made you think, "Me too!"? What did someone share that helped you see something in a brand-new way?*

Carryover Coaching
Use these additional prompts for one-on-one conferences.
- Think about the moments when the character experienced bias and sought support to take action.
- Write down the importance of the actions and consequences.

📖 Beyond the Book

We learned how important it is to recognize bias and misunderstandings and to take action for justice. This beautiful story demonstrates the courage and actions the main character, Kora-Jalimuso, took to teach her teacher and classmates how to pronounce her name. Our names hold an enormous role in representing our identity and who we are. With your students, read the glossary of names featured in the story at the end of the book. Select names to read aloud, review the pronunciation together, and share their origins and meaning. Have students select names and read them aloud as well. Then, invite students to design a poster with their names, pronunciation, origin, and meaning. Students can research their names or ask their caregivers for help.

SKILLS AND STANDARDS

CASEL:
Self-Awareness
- Integrate personal and social identities
- Examine prejudices and biases

A student's research on her name, its origin, and its meaning.

A Few More Favorites

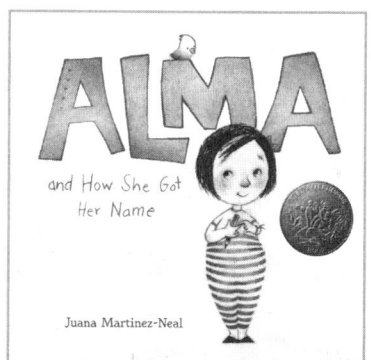

Alma and How She Got Her Name
by Juana Martinez-Neal

The Name Jar
by Yangsook Choi

THE FINAL PART

A trait many of us educators share is our love of books. We know that if we happen across a bookstore in our travels, we will be pulled into its doors. We get lost in the children's section for an eternity. Hours later, we emerge, arms loaded with new adventures for our students to get lost in, too. This is an absolute truth for us.

So, as you can imagine, narrowing down the stories to include in this resource was no easy task. The more covers we cracked open and explored, the more books we fell in love with. We wish we could have offered you even more stories. We also know that as this resource sits in your hands, more and more brand-new future favorites will fill up bookstore shelves.

The good news: The lenses and lessons can go beyond the books we've shared here. You can transfer the strategies to other texts. The thinking can and should be carried away from the mentor texts and into the books that live in our students' independent reading baggies and choice texts. So feel free to continue shopping for other books!

Bringing the Reading Lenses to the Bookstore

When seeking books for primary classrooms, we often use a mental checklist to ensure that the books we offer will be engaging, authentic, and allow children to pretend themselves into the story. While we don't walk around bookstores with a checklist in hand, here are a few things to look for as you explore the shelves.

- #OwnVoices authors
- Colorful and engaging artwork
- Clear images of facial expressions and expressive bodies
- Characters with identities that match those of children (and adults) in your classroom
- Characters with identities that offer a peek into someone else's world
- Celebrations that honor different identities
- Challenges that children can understand
- Language variety: Ways that different identity groups express themselves
- Authenticity (avoid books with tokenized or stereotypical characters)

Why We Prioritized #OwnVoices

On September 6, 2015, Corinne Duyvis created and defined #OwnVoices, a hashtag that became a movement. In a tweet, she defined #OwnVoices as texts "about diverse characters written by authors from that same diverse group" (2015). In the thread that followed, she added more clarity by stating the intent is "to lift up those who are often ignored" and to represent "all kinds of marginalized groups." Subsequently, the movement grew, and the hashtag was co-opted by the publishing industry, which turned it into a catch-all marketing phrase that eventually blurred its original meaning and intent. Although this resulted in the organization We Need Diverse Books deciding to cease use of the term, we have chosen to center #OwnVoices—as it was originally intended—in our work.

Picture books contain two messages—one by the author and one by the illustrator. Because of this, we have expanded the definition of #OwnVoices to include books in which either the author or illustrator or both hold the marginalized status of the main character(s). The book shopping "checklist" we presented earlier, as well as the content of our book, hopefully presents our belief that it is important to center historically and/or culturally marginalized voices in the texts we use to teach—not just the ones we add to the classroom library. Furthermore, we aspire to ensure each text we select satisfies two critical criteria put forth by educator Laura Jiménez:

- "It must be an authentic representation that shows marginalized individuals as whole people, living complex lives that do not adhere to the dominant White narrative."
- "It must push back against biased narratives of the community." (Jiménez, 2021).

Creating Your Own Strategies

One goal of this resource is to give teachers a few ready-to-go lessons to have at their fingertips. We know what it is like to have so much to plan and not enough time to plan it! However, we don't believe that you have to teach the strategies and lessons we've provided exactly as we've laid them out or with the mentor texts we've selected. We hope that you will come up with your own authentic strategies for your teaching as well. Unpacking your own process will allow you to use the texts we've centered in new ways. A fun and fruitful way to create your own strategies is to spy on yourself as a reader and notice how your own brain works to comprehend and think about the text. If you're planning to create your own strategies, here's a mini guide to help you bring your thinking process to life for your readers.

> **A Strategy for Strategy Making**
> **1.** Choose a skill and practice doing it in your mentor text (e.g., identify a character trait).
> **2.** Ask yourself: *How did I just do that? What did I look at, ask myself, or think about?*
> **3.** Put your process into a few actionable steps.

If you are carrying a strategy into another text, go back to the steps. Think about a place in the new book that would fit the strategy. Then, bring yourself through the steps to plan out your modeling and think-aloud for children.

Circles for Change in Your School Community

Our invitation with the stories and lessons in this resource is to shift our practice to make it student-centered. In doing so, we aim to reach all individuals by creating a space and experience to feel seen, heard, and understood. We extend our work to take the necessary steps toward identity, healing, and heartwork. This book serves as an invitation for educators, children, and the community alike. We know these conversations are crucial. Our next questions are: *How do we begin? How do we hear from the voices that have not been heard yet?*

Throughout this book, we present numerous examples of restorative practices and circle conversations to engage in with children. We can utilize the same practices with adults as well. Our adult-to-adult conversations might be between groups of educators, between educators and parents, or among educators and PTO leadership. Ultimately, we might have these conversations when we find ourselves in an opportune position to engage with any other stakeholder within our educational institutions. Among colleagues, these circle conversations can extend to faculty meetings, professional learning communities (PLCs), and collaborative partnerships across grade levels, subject matters, districts, and states. Among stakeholders, these conversations can occur within board of education meetings, parent presentations, and back-to-school nights. We can use the design and implementation of circle conversations or book clubs to guide and support this work together.

We recognize that sometimes there are a very limited number of opportunities, if any, for this type of connection and conversation. We acknowledge that spaces defined by a culture of toxicity, resistance, and isolation do exist. We also realize that many of us might feel alone in this work. For those of us educators who are seeking a community of partners and collaborators, there fortunately exists an extensive support system within larger educational groups. You can find these through social media, educational blogs, and collaborative teaching institutions, to name just a few. We want to assure you that you don't have to feel alone in your work with this text and that there are always partnerships available for support and collaboration.

Taking a moment to honor and recognize the various stages you might find yourself in with this work, we want to share some "go-to" resources you might use when starting up the conversation with stakeholders, regardless of where you might be on this path.

- "The 60-Second Confrontation Model" from *Fierce Conversations*, by Susan Scott (https://resources.finalsite.net/images/v1571246492/psesdorg/flklvf6unbeqi0muplzc/Confrontation-Model-Fierce-Conversation.pdf)
- *Let's Talk!* from Learning for Justice (https://www.learningforjustice.org/magazine/publications/lets-talk)
- Knoster Model for Managing Complex Change (https://blog.edsmart.com/managing-change-in-schools-a-helpful-framework)

NOTES FROM THE AUTHORS

A Note From Dana

As a White, cisgendar female, my childhood was full of storybook characters who looked like me. I befriended Beverly Cleary's Ramona and considered myself one of the girls from The Baby-Sitters Club series. Then, as I got a bit older, Judy Blume's Margaret and Katherine taught me important lessons about growing up and first loves. Belonging and mirrors were not a problem for me, as everywhere I looked I found reflections of myself on library shelves. So, why do I still feel like I missed something vital in my early reading life? I've come to believe that it is because while my childhood had wall-to-wall mirroring, there wasn't a single window to be found. The stories I loved, and continue to love, were wonderful. But they didn't offer me opportunities to see worlds, experiences, and beautiful people who didn't look like me, and collectively sent a hidden message of white superiority that I am continuously working to unlearn.

I don't blame my teachers. I was lucky to have had many wonderful educators who gave love freely and were always looking to create community. I do, however, acknowledge that our educational community is and has been well aware of how the lack of representation in our classroom libraries "others" students and sends messages that they don't belong, while also creating missed opportunities to learn about one another.

This is what pushed me to collaborate and write this book with my two amazing coauthors, Jigisha Vyas and Keisha Smith-Carrington. I am deeply grateful for their mentorship and the ways that this writing has moved me forward on my own journey toward anti-biased and antiracist teaching practices. This particular journey will be lifelong.

Contributing to this book is one step along the way. My mentor and colleague Gravity Goldberg often says that we write what we need to learn and hear. This feels especially true for me in coauthoring this project. I hope that this resource is what you needed as well, and that it can be one part of your learning journey as we move forward together to create classrooms that both center our shared humanity and celebrate the beauty of our unique identities.

A Note From Keisha

Most educators can easily name one or more books that were their favorite(s) when they were children. I cannot. Instead of one or more books, I can name the context in which books were read to me as my earliest memories of reading. In my mind, it was an every-night occurrence, although I am pretty sure this is a child's recollection. I know for a fact that the readings involved my maternal grandmother, Shirley.

Grandma Shirley and my mom (Sheila Smith) each worked separate shifts at the post office. As a manager, my grandmother worked days. This meant that most nights I was at my grandmother's house at bedtime. After tucking me in bed, she would pull from a collection of books and read to me with perfect prosody. I don't know who enjoyed this routine more—her or me. I remember warmth. I remember laughter. I remember being centered.

As an adult, I do not remember ever having any character in any of the books we read reflect me. It wasn't until I was a mother developing my children's library of bedtime and other-time readings that I discovered the works of authors like Eloise Greenfield. I do not have enough space to share the effect of seeing my name—albeit with another spelling—in her book *My Doll, Keshia*. But that feeling, combined with the effect of seeing Jan Gilchrist's illustrations of brown-skinned girls rocking Afro puffs, compelled me to include representation and cultural relevance in my home and classroom libraries.

My experiences as a reader, mother, and teacher have allowed me to witness the impact of texts on children who hold many identities. Being able to bring these older experiences and the more recent learning I've done with colleagues in my professional home into this work with Dana and Jigisha has been a wonderful experience. I am grateful for the learning community we've formed and am excited about the many educators who will join us in bringing this work to more children.

A Note From Jigisha

Growing up as a little Brown girl who identifies as Indian American and as a child of immigrants, I recall running my fingers across the spines of books on the shelves in my elementary school's library. My eyes were constantly searching for a book that would intrigue and engage my young mind and heart. As a child, I was drawn to adventure. Having been inspired by stories of trailblazing women such as Amelia Earhart, I yearned to read stories that featured characters who were driven by their curiosities and dreams.

I remember the day I discovered and developed an interest in reading the Cam Jansen series. The books feature a fifth-grade female protagonist with photographic memory who embarks on numerous adventures with her best friend to solve a slew of mysteries. I would read through the pages in class and then go on adventures with my friends after school to solve our own versions of "mysteries." One of our favorites included the use of invisible ink and a "missing" stuffed Dalmatian dog.

I vividly recall the moment I found myself observing the cover of the Cam Jansen books. They featured a little White girl with red hair, who looked very similar to all the other characters I had seen in the books that lined our library's shelves. I would search through the stories to see if there were any books with characters who looked like me, had a name like mine, or celebrated the same holidays as me. I didn't know it then, but I would spend the next 20 years waiting to discover a children's book in which I could finally see myself. I'd wait 20 years for little Brown girls everywhere to finally be seen.

My 2-year-old niece, Mia, is bright, joyful, and has a deep love for reading. She lights up our world! She has engaged with books and stories since she was only a few weeks old. Recently, Mia and I were immersed in reading the book *My Bindi,* by Gita Varadarajan. This heartwarming story is about a little Brown girl named Divya and her journey to finding empowerment and pride in her Indian American heritage, particularly in finding strength and love in her family as she proudly wears her *bindi.* As we turned the pages of the story, Mia would point to Divya's character and happily say "Mia" on each single page. My heart was so full from watching my niece be able to see herself in this story and feel seen. We then proceeded to decorate ourselves with elaborate *bindis* and celebrate the beauty of the moment.

I am confident that readers can share this experience across all reading spaces with the lessons and stories featured in this resource. Having the fortunate opportunity to coauthor this book with Dana and Keisha, I feel a deep and immense gratitude and have a great sense of hope and joy for these special moments to happen for young hearts and minds everywhere.

ACKNOWLEDGMENTS

From Dana

Every choice we make means saying yes to some things and saying no to others. Every time I said yes to making space for writing, I may have been saying no to watching one of my sons' hockey games or swim meets, cuddling up on the couch sandwiched between beautiful boys to watch a favorite show, or being the caregiver in charge of that night's dinner or homework help. Of course, there were many times when the writing got a no and my family got the yes, but my contributions to this project wouldn't have been possible without the constant understanding, support, and encouragement of my amazing partner in life, Yuma Clark, and my two wonderful children, John and Tommy. Yuma, you are the best human I know and will forever be the best choice of my life. John and Tommy, you are my heart. Writing this has been in part to make sure that children like you see themselves and their histories in their classroom experiences. Thank you for giving me the best job of my life, being your mother. And thank you to all my family and friends who may have seen a bit less of me but were there to celebrate good days and hold space and support for me on the hard ones.

In addition to home family support, my educational family has been instrumental from the beginning. Thank you to my GG LLC teammates—Gravity Goldberg, Sarah Fiedeldey, Pam Koutrakos, Heather Frank, Margy Leininger, Brianne Annitti, Christy Curran, Lily Howard Scott, Laura Sarsten, and Julie Mc Auley. Your influence lives in everything I do. To Patty McGee, Steve Fiedeldey, and Wendy Murray, without you this version of the book would still be buried deep in Google Drive. Thank you for your inspiration and support. I love you all. Thank you to my dear friends at The Curious Reader in Glen Rock, New Jersey. When it comes to helping me find new books to bring into my teaching and my home, you are my people. I also want to thank all the inspirational educators in my partner schools. I am grateful to learn with and from all of you. A special thanks goes out to East Hanover's Jackie Happich, Kasey Kaisershot, and Theresa Dathe, who tested our lessons and opened up their classrooms as playful learning spaces. Your classroom communities are examples of the beautiful and welcoming spaces we all dream of. And last but not least, to volunteer kiddos—Mili, Shaked, Tom, and their families. Our little crew helped us refine some of our lessons, and their light and the laughter we shared brought so much joy into my world.

One last thank you goes out to a whole different family—my writing friends. A great big thank you to the folks at Teach Write with Jennifer Laffin. Many pages were born during Time to Write sessions. And an especially big dollop of love to my feedback fam—Kerry Chapman, Tracy Vogelgesang, and Michelle Sheehan. You ladies have been so much more than writing support. Thank you for your honest feedback, but mostly for your friendship. I adore you.

From Keisha

I would not be the reader I am today if it weren't for my Grandma Shirley, who modeled being a voracious reader. She took her last breath the season before I agreed to write this resource and would have been extremely excited and proud that her actions contributed to me becoming an author.

In addition to my maternal grandmother, I am grateful for my adult-ren, Avey and Ashby. Each of them continues to affect the ways I look at texts. Each of them still impacts my social and emotional development. Each of them helped me, during a very difficult year, to persist through the end of my contributions to this book.

In my current professional home, there are folks whose approaches to working with children have greatly affected my practice over the last four years. These include my teammates in leading the district's equity learning (Thomas Foley, Dawn Henderson, Liz Lien, Patty Manhart, and Jen Simon) and Gita Varadarajan, a thought partner always opening her classroom as a space in which we help each other hone skills related to this book.

Beyond my professional home, there are the visionary leaders of the Institute for Racial Equity in Literacy (IREL)—Dr. Sonja Cherry-Paul and Tricia Ebarvia—and the many folks in the community they cultivate with facilitators (Aeriale, Anna, Michelle, Min, Tiana, and many more), participants (like Clare, who expanded my thinking on the intersectional use of picture books by introducing me to her work with Lynsey, Franki, and Dr. Jiménez), and keynote speakers (like Dr. Sealey-Ruiz, whose Racial Literacy Development Theory and loving ways of being now ground my praxis).

From Jigisha

Throughout my life, my mother's wisdom has echoed in my mind and has remained in my heart. She taught me to always allow myself to be open to life's unfoldings and invitations. In those moments when it feels like a number of doors are closing, there is purpose and intention leading you to the ones that will be open for you. These words have led me to have transformative experiences and have manifested a deep sense of gratitude for each singular moment.

My parents, Kishor and Kokila, have been the guiding lights throughout my life. Leaving their home country of India, my parents immigrated to the United States in their late 20s. They left behind their families, homes, and a familiar world for one that is new, unfamiliar, exciting, and different, and they navigated the journey of building their home and their lives here. The leaps they took, the experiences they endured, the trials and errors they navigated were all centered on creating opportunity for their children. They made personal sacrifices, including overnight shifts, numerous jobs, discontinuing a pursuit to further their careers, and not spending money on themselves to save for their children's violin lessons, dance classes, and basketball camps. Their time, love, energy, and sacrifices have made it possible for doors to open for me. Their wisdom—a collection of messages and support that is both grounding and uplifting; a combination of their stories and those of my grandparents, great-grandparents, and ancestors; and a wonderful mix of encouragement and enlightenment—continues to transform my life daily and will shine its light on the generations to come. To my parents—who are my protectors, my guardians, my lifelong teachers, and my friends—words are not enough to express my love, gratitude, and appreciation for you both.

To my husband, Ashish—this project could not have been possible without you. Your unwavering love, support, and encouragement have made this dream a reality for me. I am grateful for all the moments you have been my thinking partner, my sounding board, and the person who brings laughter and light into my life, especially after some of the longer days of writing. You are my best friend, the answer to a thousand prayers, and a constant supporter of my wildest dreams. Thank you for always encouraging me and reminding me about the purpose and intention of this work, for grounding me in the reasons I was called to be an educator, and for being my inspiration to leave this world a little bit better than we found it.

Every encounter and interaction leave us with a seed that is the foundation of learning and growth. I am so deeply thankful to my family and friends, who have shared stories, smiles, laughter, and tears as we talked about our own personal moments when we felt truly understood. Each of you is an inspiration for this book. And here's a final note of gratitude for the moments of connection with all my students, my teachers, and my fellow educators: Thank you for reminding me each day that we cannot stop transforming our world for children to feel seen, heard, and safe; for students to feel cared for, loved, and supported; and for students to have an infinite number of doors open for them.

From All of Us
Schools
This book truly could not have come to life until we were able to move the work from the ideas that existed in our minds into real-life lesson work in classrooms with little humans. There are so many awesome educators who helped us put theories into practice and refine our ideas. Special thanks go out to the leaders of all our partner schools across New York and New Jersey. Specifically, thank you to Princeton Public Schools, East Hanover Public Schools, and Wyckoff Public Schools and to all of their amazing teachers who tried out the work and opened their hearts and their classrooms to us.

Scholastic
AND OF COURSE . . . a giant thank you to the folks at Scholastic. To our fabulous editor, Maria L. Chang, we are eternally grateful for your flexibility and love, as well as for offering thoughtful and generous feedback with a smile. To Trent Hanover, for answering every question and creating comfort in our partnership. To Tannaz Fassihi, we are so grateful to partner with you in making the cover everything we could have hoped for and more. To Shelley Griffin and Samantha Unger, thank you for hearing us speak about our work and sharing it with a larger audience. To Bobby McCabe, we are so grateful and awed by the ways that you design tools to perfectly match our team's vision. To Annie Stubbs and Jacqueline Biltucci, thank you for helping us launch our stories and share our book on a broader scale. To Tara Welty, for believing in and supporting our work. And to Michelle Kim, for seeing our vision and bringing life to our ideas on the page. Thank you to the Scholastic team for your support and for your belief in us and this book.

RESOURCES

Achor, S. (2011). *The happiness advantage: The seven principles that fuel success and performance at work.* Virgin.

Achor, S. (2018). *Big potential.* Crown.

Ahmed, S. K. (2018). *Being the change: Lessons and strategies to teach social comprehension.* Heinemann.

Arnsten, A. F. (2015). "Stress weakens prefrontal networks: Molecular insults to higher cognition." *Nature Neuroscience, 18*(10), 1376.

Bidol, P. A. (1972). *Developing new perspectives on race: An innovative multi-media social studies curriculum in racism awareness for the secondary level.* New Perspectives on Race.

Bishop, R. S. (1990). "Mirrors, windows, and sliding glass doors." In H. Moir (Ed.), *Collected perspectives: Choosing and using books for the classroom, 6*(3). Christopher-Gordon Publishers

Brackett, M. A. (2020). *Permission to feel: The power of emotional intelligence to achieve well-being and success.* Celadon Books.

Brown, B. (2012). *Listening to shame.* TED Talks. Retrieved March 28, 2022, from https://www.ted.com/talks/brene_brown_listening_to_shame?language=en

Brown, B. (2015). *Daring greatly: How the courage to be vulnerable transforms the way we live, love, parent, and lead.* Avery.

Brown, B. (2022). *Atlas of the heart: Mapping meaningful connection and the language of human experience.* Random House.

Bucci, D., Cannon, A., & Ramkarran, A. (2017, September). "Community, Circles and Collaboration: The First 10 Days." https://www.iirp.edu/images/pdf/RsmGIW_Restorative_Approaches-_First_10_Days_1.pdf

Calkins, L. (2001). *The art of teaching reading.* Longman.

CASEL. (2017a). "Examples of social and emotional learning in elementary English language arts instruction." Retrieved from https://casel.s3.us-east-2.amazonaws.com/SEL-in-Elementary-ELA-8-20-17.pdf

CASEL. (2017b). "Sample teaching activities to support core competencies of social and emotional learning." Retrieved from https://casel.s3.us-east-2.amazonaws.com/Sample-Teaching-Activities-to-Support-Core-Competencies.pdf

CASEL. (2020a). "CASEL'S SEL framework: What are the core competence areas and where are they promoted?" Retrieved from https://casel.s3.us-east-2.amazonaws.com/CASEL-SEL-Framework-11.2020.pdf

CASEL. (2020b). CASEL CARES webinar series: SEL as a lever for equity and social justice – Part II: Adult SEL to support antiracist practices. Retrieved from https://casel.org/events/sel-as-a-lever-for-equity-part-two/

Center for Early Childhood Mental Health Consultation. (n.d.). *Ideas for teaching children about emotions.* https://www.ecmhc.org/ideas/emotions.html

Cherng, H. Y. (2016). "Is all classroom conduct equal?: Teacher contact with parents of racial/ethnic minority and immigrant adolescents." *Teachers College Record, 118*(11), 1–32. Retrieved from https://www.tcrecord.org ID Number: 21625.

Children's Community School. (2018). They're not too young to talk about race! Retrieved from http://www.childrenscommunityschool.org/wp-content/uploads/2018/02/theyre-not-too-young-1.pdf

Chugh, D. (2018). *The person you mean to be: How good people fight bias.* HarperCollins.

Clark, K. B., & Clark, M. P. (1947). "Racial identification and preference in negro children." In T. M. Newcomb & E. L. Hartley (Eds.), *Readings in social psychology* (602– 611). Holt, Rinehart & Winston. Retrieved from https://i2.cdn.turner.com/cnn/2010/images/05/13/doll.study.1947.pdf

Cobb, F., & Krownapple, J. (2019). *Belonging through a culture of dignity: The keys to successful equity implementation.* Mimi and Todd Press.

Costello, B., Wachtel, J., & Wachtel, T. (2019). *Restorative circles in schools: A practical guide for educators.* International Institute for Restorative Practices.

DeBeaumont, A., Fairbanks, I., Ahn, J., & Atwood, A. (2021). "If the world was a village of 100 people" *IdeaFest.* https://red.library.usd.edu/idea/291

Delpit, L. D. (2006). *Other people's children: Cultural conflict in the classroom.* W.W. Norton.

Derman-Sparks, L., Edwards, J. O., & Goins, C. M. (2020). *Anti-bias education for young children and ourselves,* 2nd edition. NAEYC

Duyvis, C. [@corinneduyvis]. (2015, September 6). Twitter. #ownvoices, to recommend kidlit about diverse characters written by authors from that same diverse group. https://twitter.com/corinneduyvis/status/640584099208503296

Edmondson, A. (1999). "Psychological safety and learning behavior in work teams." *Adm. Sci. Q. 44*(2):350–83

Edmondson, A. (n.d.). *Building a psychologically safe workplace.* TED Talks. Retrieved from https://www.youtube.com/watch?v=LhoLuui9gX8&ab_channel=TEDxTalks.

Emdin, C. (2017). *For white folks who teach in the hood – and the rest of Y'all too: Reality pedagogy and urban education.* Beacon Press.

Everett, C. C. (2017, November 22). "There is no diverse book." *ImagineLIT.* Retrieved March 28, 2022, from http://www.imaginelit.com/news/2017/11/21/there-is-no-diverse-book

Fountas, I. C., & Pinnell, G. S. (2001). *Guiding readers and writers, grades 3-6: Teaching comprehension, genre, and content literacy.* Heinneman.

Gay. G. (2010). *Culturally responsive teaching: Theory, research, and practice.* Teachers College Press.

Gender Justice in Early Childhood. (2017). "Gender in early childhood V1." [Fact sheet]. Retrieved from www.genderjusticeinearlychildhood.com

Gervais, M. (2018). *Finding mastery podcast 065: Dr. Judson Brewer.* Retrieved April 8, 2019, from https://findingmastery.net/judson-brewer/

Goldberg, G. (2016). *Mindsets & moves: Strategies that help readers take charge, grades 1–8.* Corwin.

Harro, B. (2018). The cycle of socialization. In M. Adams, W. J. Blumenfeld, D. Chase, J. Catalano, K. DeJong, H. W. Hackman, L. E. Hopkins, B. J. Love, M. L. Peters, D. Shlasko, & X Zúñiga (Eds.), *Readings for diversity and social justice.* Routledge.

Harvey, S., & Goudvis, A. (2017). *Strategies that work: Teaching comprehension for understanding, engagement, and building knowledge, grades K–8.* Stenhouse.

Hattie, J. (2018). Visible Learning[Plus]: 250+ influences on student achievement. https://visible-learning.org/wp-content/uploads/2018/03/VLPLUS-252-Influences-Hattie-ranking-DEC-2017.pdf

hooks, bell. (2018). *All about love: New visions.* William Morrow.

Husband, T. (2011). "'I don't see color': Challenging assumptions about discussing race with young children." *Early Childhood Education Journal, 39,* 365–371. https://doi.org/10.1007/s10643-011-0458-9

Jiménez, L. (2021). "Mirrors and windows with texts and readers: Intersectional social justice at work in the classroom." *Language Arts, 98*(3), 156–161.

Kirwan Institute for the Study of Race and Ethnicity. (2018). "Implicit bias module series." Retrieved from http://kirwaninstitute.osu.edu/implicit-bias-training/

Ladson-Billings, G. (2021). "I'm here for the hard re-set: Post pandemic pedagogy to preserve our culture." *Equity & Excellence in Education, 54*(1), 68–78 https://doi.org/10.1080/10665684.2020.1863883

Lawrence-Brown, D., & Sapon-Shevin, M. (2014). *Condition critical: Key principles for equitable and inclusive education.* Teachers College Press.

LeaderFactor. (n.d.). *The complete guide to psychological safety.* Retrieved from https://www.leaderfactor.com/resources/what-is-psychological-safety.

Learning for Justice. (2005). "Speak up! Responding to everyday bigotry." Retrieved from https://www.learningforjustice.org/sites/default/files/2021-05/Speak-Up-2021.pdf

Learning for Justice. (2018). "Social justice standards: The teaching tolerance anti-bias framework." https://www.learningforjustice.org/sites/default/files/2020-09/TT-Social-Justice-Standards-Anti-bias-framework-2020.pdf

Learning for Justice. (2018). "Speak up at school: How to respond to everyday prejudice, bias and stereotypes." Retrieved from https://www.learningforjustice.org/sites/default/files/2019-04/TT-Speak-Up-Guide.pdf

Learning for Justice. (2019). "Let's talk: A guide to facilitating critical conversations with students." Montgomery: The Southern Poverty Law Center. Retrieved from https://www.learningforjustice.org/sites/default/files/2021-11/LFJ-2111-Lets-Talk-November-2021-11172021.pdf

Lieberman. M. (2014). "The social brain and its superpowers." Retrieved from https://www.youtube.com/watch?v=H6L3UMlpn78&ab_channel=BrightSightSpeakers

Madda, M. J. (2019, May 15). "Dena Simmons: Without context, social-emotional learning can backfire." *EdSurge.* https://www.edsurge.com/news/2019-05-15-dena-simmons-without-context-social-emotional-learning-can-backfire

Mar, R. A. & Oatley, K. (2008). The function of fiction is the abstraction and simulation of Social Experience. *Perspectives on Psychological Science, 3*(3), 173–192.

McIntosh, P. (1989). "White privilege: Unpacking the invisible knapsack and some notes for facilitators." Retrieved from https://nationalseedproject.org/Key-SEED-Texts/white-privilege-unpacking-the-invisible-knapsack

Mentor, M., & Sealey-Ruiz, Y. (2021). "Doing the deep work of antiracist pedagogy: Toward self-excavation for equitable classroom teaching." *Language Arts, 99*(1).

Miller, D. (2013). *Reading with meaning: Teaching comprehension in the primary grades.* Stenhouse.

Moore, E., Michael, A., Penick-Parks, M. W., Singleton, G. E., & Hackman, H. (2018). *The guide for white women who teach black boys: Understanding, connecting, respecting.* Corwin.

Mraz, K., & Hertz, C. (2015). *A mindset for learning: Teaching the traits of joyful, independent growth.* Heinemann.

Muhammad, G. (2020). *Cultivating genius: An equity framework for culturally and historically responsive literacy.* Scholastic.

Nathanson, D. L. (1994). *Shame and pride: Affect, sex, and the birth of the self.* W.W. Norton.

Niemi, K. (2020, December 15). "Niemi: CASEL is updating the most widely recognized definition of social-emotional learning. Here's why." *The 74.* https://www.the74million.org/article/niemi-casel-is-updating-the-most-widely-recognized-definition-of-social-emotional-learning-heres-why/

Nieto, S. (1999). *The light in their eyes: Creating multicultural learning communities.* Teachers College Press.

Paris, D., & Alim, H. S. (2017). *Culturally sustaining pedagogies: Teaching and learning for justice in a changing world.* Teacher's College Press.

Pranis, K. (2005). *The little book of circle processes: A new/old approach to peacemaking.* Good Books.

Price-Dennis, D., & Sealey-Ruiz, Y. (2021). *Advancing racial literacies in teacher education: Activism for equity in digital spaces.* Teachers College Press.

Project Implicit. (n.d.). "Implicit association test." Retrieved from https://implicit.harvard.edu/implicit/selectatest.html

Purcell-Gates, V. (2002). "'… As soon as she opened her mouth!': Issues of language, literacy, and power". In L. D. Delpit, & J. K. Dowdy (Eds.), *The skin that we speak: Thoughts on language and culture in the classroom.* New Press.

Riess, H. (2018). *Empathy effect: Seven neuroscience-based keys for transforming the way we live, love, work, and connect across differences.* Sounds True.

Rosenblatt, L. M. (1986). "The aesthetic transaction." *Journal of Aesthetic Education, 20* (4).

Sauer, J. (2014). "Multiple identities, shifting landscapes." In D. Lawrence-Brown & M. Sapon-Shevin, *Condition critical: Key principles for equitable and inclusive education.* Teachers College.

Schulte-Cooper, L. (Fall 2015). "Awards that celebrate diversity in children's literature." *Children and Libraries.* http://dia.ala.org/sites/default/files/resources/awards-diversity.pdf

Sealey-Ruiz, Y. (2021). "The critical literacy of race: Toward racial literacy in urban teacher education." In H. R. Milner IV & K. Lomotey (Eds.), *Handbook of Urban Education, 2nd ed.* Routledge.

Sealey-Ruiz, Y. (n.d.). Archaeology of Self™. Retrieved from https://www.yolandasealeyruiz.com/archaeology-of-self

Serravallo, J. (2010). *Teaching reading in small groups: Differentiated instruction for building strategic, independent readers.* Heinemann.

Serravallo, J. (2015). *The reading strategies book: Your everything guide to developing skilled readers.* Heinemann.

Simmons, D. (2019). "Why we can't afford whitewashed social-emotional learning." *Education Update, 61*(4).

Simmons, D. (2021). "Why SEL alone isn't enough." *Educational Leader, 78*(6).

Stevenson, H. C. (2014). *Promoting racial literacy in schools.* Teachers College Press.

Stevenson, H. C. (2017). *How to resolve racially stressful situations.* TED Talks. Retrieved from https://tedmed.com/talks/show?id=691362.

Tatum, B. D. (2000). The complexity of identity: "Who am I?." In M. Adams, W. J. Blumenfeld, H. W. Hackman, X. Zuniga, & M. L. Peters (Eds.), *Readings for diversity and social justice: An anthology on racism, sexism, anti-semitism, heterosexism, classism and ableism* (pp. 9–14). Routledge.

Tatum, B. D. (2017). *"Why are all the black kids sitting together in the cafeteria?": And other conversations about race.* Basic Books.

Terrell, R. D., & Lindsey, R. B. (2009). *Culturally proficient leadership: The personal journey begins within.* Corwin.

Wachtel, T. (2013). *Dreaming of a new reality: How restorative practices reduce crime and violence, improve relationships and strengthen civil society.* The Piper's Press.

Walther, M. P. (2019). *The ramped-up read aloud: What to notice as you turn the page.* Corwin Literacy.

We Need Diverse Books. https://diversebooks.org

"Wheel of emotions." *Defend Innocence.* https://defendinnocence.org/wp-content/uploads/2019/02/DI_EmotionWheel-v02.pdf

Winfrey, O., & Perry, B. D. (2022). *What happened to you?: Conversations on trauma, resilience, and healing.* Bluebird.

Wiseman, T. (2019). "Theresa Wiseman's four attributes of empathy." Retrieved https://scarlettstrategic.com.au/2019/08/24/theresa-wisemans-four-attributes-of-empathy/